DISCARD

Successful African-American Men
From Childhood to Adulthood

SUCCESSFUL AFRICAN-AMERICAN MEN
From Childhood to Adulthood

Sandra Taylor Griffin, Ph.D.

*A dissertation submitted to
the Graduate Faculty in Psychology and
accepted as a requirement for the degree of Doctor of Philosophy
The City University of New York*

KLUWER ACADEMIC / PLENUM PUBLISHERS
New York, Boston, Dordrecht, London, Moscow

ISBN 0-306-46363-6

©2000 Kluwer Academic / Plenum Publishers, New York
233 Spring Street, New York, N.Y. 10013

http://www.wkap.nl/

10 9 8 7 6 5 4 3 2 1

A C.I.P. record for this book is available from the Library of Congress.

All rights reserved

No part of this book may be reproduced, stored in a retrieval system, or transmitted
in any form or by any means, electronic, mechanical, photocopying, microfilming, recording,
or otherwise, without written permission from the Publisher

Printed in the United States of America

PREFACE

When one reviews the literature, the background experiences of dysfunctional black men are often explored while few studies examine the motivating triggers for high achieving black men. The research purpose was to reveal the nurturing behavioral settings that high achieving black men used as adolescents and examine whether social capital played a role in helping them negotiate their way out of disadvantage. Thus, how black male adolescents reared in disadvantaged black communities were prepared to have high achieving adult outcomes was investigated. Additionally explored was what role adolescent community settings played in the men's success process. And, more importantly, how did settings accommodate the men's diversity, complexity, and the influence of black culture, and reconcile it to their being responsive to, and able to cope with mainstream America.

The findings support the theoretical construct of Coleman (1988) which argues that effective socialization relies in part on what happens outside the family. Participants for the study were 28 high achieving Black men between the ages of 28 and 77. It was hypothesized that for achievement oriented black male adolescents, a community of like-minded individuals were needed to expand and support their positive goal direction. The results showed the black male adolescent becomes increasingly aware of the world's dimensions, reality, fantasies and possibilities through their person-environment interactional processes. The main context is that, for them, their "life spaces" (environmental interactions) were nested in (a) self, (b) family and home, (c) the neighborhood (peers and adult influences), (d) the black community and (e) their adolescent settings. What is particularly important is that, in turn, these settings were able to act as "refuges from racism" to validate the youths' value, teach them the rules and skills of survival and expand their opportunities within an interconnected web of positive reinforcing community influences.

It is hoped that this research will sensitize psychologists, sociologists and others to the diversity found within communities of color and generate more studies on the complexities of black men and their communities.

ACKNOWLEDGMENTS

First and foremost, I want to express my deepest appreciation to the men of this dissertation, who generously opened up their lives and feelings to me. This study could not have been successfully executed without their honest responses and cooperation and we are all richer for their willingness to be so candid. The greatest debt though is to Dr. Susan Saegert, my dissertation chair, who championed the dissertation's comprehensiveness and relevance and provided guidance and insights as I struggled to make sense of the data. Her direction, editorial leadership, trust in me and encouragement over the years were invaluable and from her guidance I grew tremendously as a researcher. A special thanks to Dr. Anderson J. Franklin and Dr. Pamela Reid, of my dissertation committee for their ongoing commitment and support. Certain ideas in the work they contributed, sparked over the years in my conversations with them and after they exposed me to the writings of significant Black scholars. They also taught me how to tell the men's story in an exciting way and to make the broader conceptualizations. My gratitude is also to Dr. Roscoe C. Brown and Dr. John Cardwell, who took the time to read, edit and give freely of their time and insights in the later stages of my work.

This dissertation is dedicated to my parents, the late James D. and Nora Hobson Taylor. Their love, support and belief that I could do anything, led me to this moment from my early beginnings. It is also dedicated to my husband, Percy Griffin for providing an unending source of support. He was there with me from the beginning, encouraging me to never give up and helping me in a variety of ways during the many stages of my research. I thank my daughter, Kammara for her encouragement and for putting up with my late nights and the other oddities of having a mother "in school". And, a special thanks to Kathleen Gaynor and Marie Martin for their patience, assistance, diligence and especially support in the typing of this document. Lastly, I thank God for giving me the strength to persevere.

CONTENTS

1 INTRODUCTION	1
1.1 Statement of the Problem	2
2. LITERATURE REVIEW	5
2.1 The Factors within Community That Discourage Adolescent from Achieving	5
2.2 The Factors within Community That Encourage Adolescents to Achieve	6
2.3 Adolescents and the Environment: Basic Issues	7
2.4 Adolescence As a Time of Rapid Developmental Change	8
2.5 Lewin's Theory of Psychological "Life Space"	8
2.6 Barker's Theory of Behavioral Settings	9
2.7 Theoretical Rationale	9
2.8 Conceptual Framework	10
3 METHODS	13
3.1 Research Procedure	13
3.2 Description of the Research Instrumentation	16
4 CASE PROFILES	21
4.1 Introduction of Case Profiles	21
5 DISCUSSION OF RESULTS	49
5.1 The Role of the Men's Adolescent Neighborhoods in the Socialization Process	51
5.2 The Role of Family in the Men's Adolescent Socialization Process	56
5.3 Mother's Role	59
5.4 Other Factors Related to Place Use	62
5.5 Academic Levels: School Environment	66
5.6 The Impact of Racism on the Socialization Process	69
6 THE ADOLESCENT SETTINGS	73
6.1 Recollections of the Most Influential Settings Used	73
6.2 Setting Types Further Explored	77
6.3 The Utilization and Role of Significant Adults and Peers in the Settings	80
6.4 Men's Reasons For Using Settings and the Lessons They Learned There	84
7 HOW THE MEN FELT THEIR BEHAVIOR CHANGED AFTER USING THEIR SETTINGS	91
7.1 Developed A New Sense of Self	92
7.2 Opened Up Awareness of a Society They Wanted To Be In	92
7.3 Gained New Socialization and Friendship Skills	94

	7.4 Recognized That The World Has Rules and Respected Them	94
8 CONCLUSION		97
	8.1 Review of the Research Purpose and Objectives	97
	8.2 Summary of Findings	97
	8.3 Limits of the Study	106
	8.4 Implications for Future Research	107

APPENDIX 1
    DEMOGRAPHICS   109

APPENDIX 2
    FOCUS GROUP INSTRUMENTS   119

APPENDIX 3
    PARTICIPANT INSTRUMENTS   123

BIBLIOGRAPHY   129

1 INTRODUCTION

What do we know about Black men's adolescent community settings in disadvantaged communities? The purpose of this dissertation is to examine the role Black men's adolescent settings played as early motivational influences in their adult outcomes.

Little is known about the Black man's relationship to his disadvantaged community but social scientists virtually all agree that his family life plays a critical role in his outcome. Essentially, they emphasize the presence of a mother in the home as a major factor in the kinds of future he chooses. Yet, there are many reasons to suggest that there may be other potential variables that contribute to his achievement. These influences instill in the adolescent a positive self image and include: the parents and other family member's expectations, the youth's own self concept and confidence, the support networks available for goal orientation and the active coping activities available outside of his home (Garbarino, 1992; Larson, 1984). In this chapter, of particular importance to me is to define the settings outside his home that support adolescent males, especially his adolescent settings.

The works of black scholars (Lefcourt, 1982) conclude that the black male adolescent cannot be thought about without thinking about the black community or black group associations. These works establish that among individual black children self-image arises through their individual community interactions and supports. Thus, the black child learns to assume the roles and attitudes of others with whom he interacts and with secure attachments, they are able to tolerate frustration, and gain self-esteem and self-confidence. The social influence of others (individuals or organizations) within black communities may convey the appropriate value orientation for black adolescents to achieve (Banks, 1978; Garbarino, 1992). Indeed, if this external validation occurs, it seems reasonable to assume achievement directed aspirations for black adolescents can be derived from black community settings. These settings can become important influences in providing the supportive group climate that is itself a source of resilience (Garbarino, 1992).

Central to the argument is that the typical black child whether urban or rural spends his formative years, in point of fact, in a black world (Baughman, 1972). Rohrer and Edmonson (1964) in their study of black adolescents found that the adult choices for job or future always have strong precursors in the disadvantaged adolescent's experiences. Thus, it is the aid of his community, which provides him with a strong sense of self. And it is his disadvantaged community, which provides him with his frame of reference to convince him that he is someone special and motivates his achievement. In turn the adolescent may employ community settings as nurturing supports where his potential and goal direction may bloom (Garbarino, 1992).

The dissertation examines high achieving black men's adolescent settings to determine whether there were specific examples of commonly experienced settings that instilled the values of success, dedication, commitment and excellence and to explore the critical relationships between the youths and their settings that eventually made them the men they became. As a logical consequence; my investigation frames broad questions about how these high achieving black men felt their adolescent places played a role in motivating them.

My own question became, will salient social support systems shield black adolescents from the ill effects of their disadvantaged communities and lead to a successful outcome? There was little specific research on the practical relationship between the black male adolescent, his particular nurturing settings, his adult drive for achievement and the environmental influences, which act as a causal force driving him to achieve.

The literature supports the idea that any research about minority achievement needs to be looked at more holistically. Thus, there is a need to consider the interrelationship between the individual and his environment. Then, we can begin to think about the questions central to our investigation. What are the interfaces between black adolescents, the group settings they use, and their drive to achieve?

More importantly, the research may be the basis for further, more extensive, research into the influence of community places for African American males. That is, perhaps, through descriptive case study data, we can better understand how community behavioral settings affect life paths.

As I study how community settings influence life choices, I hope to answer several questions. They are:

1. What internal factors contribute to black adolescent males perception of their environment as supportive, and in what ways does this perception influence their pursuit of goals?

2. What internal factors contribute to black adolescent males perception of their environment as unsupportive and in what ways is this perception coped with?

3. How does the black adolescent male's environmental experience influence his sense of self and empower him to achieve as a desired goal?

This research is not a study of adolescents, rather it is a study of adults who look back on their adolescence and remember the places in their communities that strongly influenced their development.

1.1 STATEMENT OF THE PROBLEM

It is evident that no statistic is more troubling and has a more horrifying effect on the image of black men than the impact of a recent New York Times headline which read, "One In 4 Young black Men Is In Custody" (October 4, 1990, p. 6). At the same time, statistics derived from a private study of 609,690 black men in their twenties showed that they were in prison, jail, probation or parole which amounts to about 23% of the black men in that age group (Boston Globe, September 4, 1991, p. 53). Other statistics show that the homicide rate among black men is six to seven times higher than the rate for white men (<u>Times Herald Record</u>, December 4, 1993, p. 33) and 45% of black men are likely to become victims of violent crime three or four times in their life and have a life expectancy of 66 years comparable to 72.3 for white men (Duneier, 1992). At this juncture, these statistics paint a depressing picture of the prevailing image of black men as they tell us much of what we know about what it means to be a black man in America. Such is the physical surrounding of the disadvantaged community that most black men grow up in. It is a world set apart -- not so much in terms of geographical distance but in terms of the facilities and opportunities it affords its inhabitants to develop a wholesome view of themselves and sustain hope for a better tomorrow.

Much has been written about the sociology and psychology of black men, and their communities. Yet, social scientists seldom write about many other black men raised in these same stereotyped African-American[1] communities who strive for fulfilling productive lives. Deutsh (1967) and Ward (1982) in contemplating the education of disadvantaged children imply that "disadvantaged" is not a homogenous group. That is, within each group are great variations. This view is significant because it communicates that some black men as adolescents learn to be high achievers in an environment more challenging than most children face. Consequently, it reminds us that black mainstream is not a tangle of pathology. Rather it demonstrates a source for strength and resilience that is deeply rooted and viable against incredible odds. Most of all, it highlights that research on the factors that motivate black male adolescents from disadvantaged communities to achieve is needed.

The topic I chose to investigate comes out of my interest in high achieving black men's relation to communities that they grew up in; and the role that these communities played to direct them on their life paths. I attempted to examine the multiplicity of causal factors that motivate their rise above what is stereotyped as the negativity or the moral isolation sometimes presented as inherent in most black communities. Additionally, I investigated their childhood memories, different adolescent experiences, opportunities, support systems, and some personality predispositions. Essentially, the desired goal is to find out which adolescent settings contributed to nurturing their intra-personal and interpersonal coping resources and, gave them the impetus to reach their full potential.

Central to the research was to begin to understand the struggles and drive for upward mobility and to explore how a wide variety of high achieving black men would describe the settings of their communities where their early lives were formed. Beginning with a detailed history of early life youth and maturation, family background factors and personality traits and explicit places, essentially, the purpose was to examine certain features of their lives to determine whether there were commonly held experiences of community places motivating their drive to achieve. At issue was to find out whether there were places which fueled and encouraged their setting high goals, and to look for commonalties among them.

I investigated what some of the special characteristics that differentiate high achieving black adolescent's from low achieving adolescents were. Specifically I wanted to know if high achievement is a characteristic that emerges

---

[1] The term Black and African-American are used interchangeably.

in adolescence and whether it is triggered or reinforced by environmental settings. Hopefully, the themes from the men's early experiences emerge to reveal what ingredients were responsible for their achievement and what gave them a positive self image and goal direction. The study sought to determine what the men owed themselves; what they owed others or their families, and what they owed salient settings. Accordingly, I explored the places, and webs of connections they used. Then, while it seems evident that a variety of factors played a role in stimulating the black male adolescent's drive to achieve, the research asked if there were shared commonalities of influencing places? In looking for similarities of places I found that settings may act as buffers or refuges from negative feedback and influences in disadvantaged communities. Settings as identified in the study were gyms, sports teams, youth centers, clubhouses, church youth groups, street corners, and a variety of places, which the men used to gain a sense of self esteem and goal direction.

This study attempts to answer in part the question how, where, and with whom black men are encouraged to develop for security, self esteem, connection, self identity (Janowitz, 1952; Suttles, 1972; Clarke, 1983). Staples (1994) eloquently clarifies the core idea of the research when he writes:

... my inquisitor was asking me to explain my existence. Why was I successful, law abiding and literate, when others of my kind filled the jails, morgues, and homeless shelters? ... the only honest answer is the life itself. (p. 259)

What follows is a review of literature that was important to the formulation of research questions for this study.

2 LITERATURE REVIEW

2.1 THE FACTORS WITHIN COMMUNITY THAT DISCOURAGE ADOLESCENTS FROM ACHIEVING

In this section I first examined the literature on black men who fail to achieve. Overall, the literature on the causes for black men's life choices use sociological perspectives. Kotlowitz (1991), McCall (1984), Scott (1993), Monroe (1988) and Berreuta-Clement (1984) conclude that black men's life choices are attributed to their reaction to specific social conditions within their environments. The psychological offerings of Comer (1972), Majors (1992), Billson (1992), Garbarino, Dubrow, Kostelny and Pardo (1992) were promising as they describe the roots of men's adolescent behaviors and identify why they develop into volatile, angry adults. They found that while black men learn early the roles of breadwinner and hard work, they fail to attain the tangible rewards white men get. Without the means to fulfill these roles adequately, they become frustrated, impatient, angry, and embittered. More subtly, they fulfill the cycle of alienation, dysfunction and despair. Monroe (1988) advances this argument as he writes, ". . . For them the odds favoring success in the outside world was the same possibility as hitting the lotto. . .knowing the deck was stacked against them. . . accordingly, most choose not to play. . . ." Much black literature (Monroe, 1988; McCall, 1994; Johnson, 1989; Scott, 1993) traces black men's youthful lack of motivation to a general lack of hope. Johnson (1989) concludes that a great number of blacks show signs of collective depression which motivates them to select destructive alternatives. Thus, the black adolescent with a negative view of self breeds hopelessness and despair as he selects destructive life path choices (Caruthers, 1958; Johnson, 1989). It appears then, that the critical question to ask is what lies below the surface of the ideological differences between adolescents with perseverance, and those without it?

These findings frame the discussion and offer the impetus for more explicit research on the interconnectedness of negative environmental factors to one's life course. For my purposes, extensive research on what enables black adolescents to persevere and excel would be fruitful. In the next section I examine those factors that encourage achievement.

2.2 THE FACTORS WITHIN COMMUNITY THAT ENCOURAGE ADOLESCENTS TO ACHIEVE

Few studies that explore the environmental experiences of black dysfunctional adolescents take into account black adolescents who grow up to become high achieving black men. Consequently there are alarmingly few attempts to explicate the distinct factors responsible for black achievement or to understand the diversity of black groups and black geographical settings.

A review of the literature led to reflection on the familiar themes. Fundamentally, what motivates achievement? Edwards and Polite's psychological profile (1992) of the generation of black successes emerging from the cataclysmic civil rights struggle conclude that central to black adult achievement are the common experiences of youthful self affirmation, a positive sense of self and self pressure. Similar findings by Johns (1993), Staples (1994), and Ryan (1994) support that achievement is generally encouraged by individual inner patience, focus, commitment, and a positive attitude. Yet, influences of social scientists warn about the negative impact of racism on achievement. Cose (1994) describes the black adult achiever's feelings of rage and frustration. David (1969) in his study of nineteen prominent men and women points out that growing up black and exposed to violence and hatred as a result of racism can breed adult violence and hatred. But, he concludes blacks early upbringing also instills in them a desire to beat the system and succeed against racism in spite of the apparent futility of their struggle. Steele (1990) asserts that blacks can overcome any obstacle by relying on their own individual efforts to gain access into mainstream America. David's (1969) profiles of Gordon Parks, Walter White, Bill Russell, Claude Brown, Malcolm X, Dick Gregory and Richard Wright show that each man when presented with a choice to lash out bitterly and violently without reason or direction or to channel their energies into meaningful, positive efforts, chose achievement. It is a choice faced at one time or another by every black youth, even today. The black literature on black men concludes there is a connection between behavioral breakdown and the individual's inability to achieve.

It seems appropriate that if we are to identify the obstacles to achievement, we need to explore the experiences of adult achievers. In lieu of finding extensive, traditional sociological or psychological research, I closely examined the black literature (memoirs) on high achieving black men. David (1969) Cose (1994), Staples (1994) Lamar (1991) Brown (1992) Whetstone (1994) Farley (1994) and Lewis (1994) describe the community adolescent environmental settings they used for interpersonal support systems. They offer salient information on how their individual community's encouragement formed their attitudes, patterns of behavior and values. David's (1969) profile provides a poignant view of Claude Brown's boyhood in Harlem: Brown writes:

> By the time I was nine years old I had been hit by a bus, thrown into the Harlem River (intentionally), hit by a car, severely beaten with a chair and I had set a house on fire.

David concludes, what is remarkable about Brown, who went from one reform school to another, organized gang wars and was an accomplished thief, was that he went on to become a law student at one of America's leading universities, and at 28 years old wrote <u>Manchild in the Promised Land</u>.

Another such example is Les Brown's autobiography (1992). Brown described his childhood as "coming up the hard way." He was born into poverty, raised by a single mother and labeled educably "mentally retarded" as a youth.

He attributes his life path to a teacher who saw a spark in him during his adolescence and taught him the crucial lesson of controlling who he could become. Brown described his experiences joining this teacher's drama club. As an adult, with no formal education after high school, Brown became a successful disc jockey, served three terms in the Ohio legislature and became one of the country's preeminent motivational speakers for corporate America and a television star. These perspectives raise the issue of the defining values, which seem to be a requirement for achievement. Kluckjohn and Stroatbeck (1967) and Thomas (1967) define the term as the standard of desired behavior, which influences individuals to choose high achieving behavior. As such, it is plausible that instilling values could influence black male adolescents to achieve. With this focus, Parham (1989) suggests it is no wonder then that much of what black youngsters come to value positively and negatively in their world is influenced by what significant others in their life value as well.

Conversely, Ronka (1994) observes children's perceptions of adult beliefs can be an important antecedent of their own beliefs. Accordingly, as children get older during adolescence, peer influences may become the major antecedent of their value choices. And, the literature is explicit that social group support settings have served black communities well as places where values may be instilled. Lamar (1991) points out that environmental "settings" can afford a context of shared values, and identify opportunities for goal directed behavior. In his work, he observed: "My father, a self made man who rose to power grew up in terrible poverty in Jim Crow Georgia but he proudly said to me. . . I am an escapee from the garbage can." Other scholars (Staples, 1994; Clarke, 1987; Ryan, 1994), offer vivid portraits of the values that supported them and the strengths and vulnerabilities of the black communities that molded them.

These black men's reflections point out crucial lesson that black youths may not always be able to control what life puts in their path but they can control who they become. Much of the black literature suggests that these youthful achievers learn early on that there is something special in them, something good to offer and that they can make a difference in the world. When they decide to pursue success they take responsibility for their lives and become the agents of their mental, physical and material achievements.

Although black scholars mention the individuals responsible for influencing young achievers' behavior, few describe in detail the settings within which they are influenced. Based on a review of the psychological and sociological research, my notion is to investigate the idea that salient community settings can act as refuges, supports, and systems of motivation for black male adolescents in disadvantaged communities and that the settings existence is important in helping adolescents find the supportive peers and adults they need.

2.3   ADOLESCENTS AND THE ENVIRONMENT: BASIC ISSUES

This section examines the literature that addresses questions on the critical relationships between adolescents and their environment and identifies which settings within the adolescent's every day life provide meaningful social supports. In effect, we are led to ask, where does he go and what does he do to overcome the adverse influences within his community? Accordingly, we ask who administers these settings, and how are goal directed values of achievement instilled?

To arrive at the appropriate answers, I began by examining the central assumptions made about adolescence in our society and the psychological literature available about how environments become influential. A large body of the literature described community as independent from the sociological and physical variables that shape an adolescent's character. Such conclusions seemed improbable after I reviewed the works of more ecologically oriented theorists. Bronfenbrenner, 1977, 1979; Ogbu, 1981; and Vygotsky, 1978 who emphasize the role of various ecological factors in shaping the end course and end goals of adolescent development and how adolescents struggle for identity formation as cognitive changes emerge.

2.4 ADOLESCENCE AS A TIME OF RAPID DEVELOPMENTAL CHANGE

Fairly extensive studies in psychology on adolescent development were useful for my purposes. This research is quite diverse and specific in focus. The sociological works represent adolescence as a time of complex physiological changes including puberty and psychological individualization. But more importantly it is also a time for identity formation and struggles for behavioral, emotional and decisional autonomy (Damon, 1983; Elder, 1980, Muuss, 1982; Elkind, 1970). It is significant that Clark (1983) identifies adolescence as a period of inner turmoil where children shift from the child role toward the adult role. He distinguishes, ". . . fear of failure, fear of success, self doubt, uncertainty. . .are fairly normal. Will I succeed. . . will I fail. . . and what career do I want to pursue become important quandaries for adolescents as they learn to manage their lives during this critical period.

Given this focus it became necessary to lay out a way of thinking about what is a pre-condition for the adolescent's selection of his goals. That is, what prepares the adolescent for life on the right track? What difficulties does he encounter in trying to construct his daily existence through a pre-given set of structures? Can settings control behavior? And, more importantly, can adolescents develop "potentiality" through interaction with settings? (Hyram, 1972)

2.5 LEWIN'S THEORY OF PSYCHOLOGICAL "LIFE SPACE"

Against this backdrop I chose to explore the role of environmental settings in relationship to behavior. Lewin (1936) and Barker (1968) delve into the interplay that occurs between the child and his settings, how his environment influences him in the choices he makes. Lewin (1936) offers a purely psychological theory (distinct from biological or physical theories) which suggests that behavior is determined by one's psychological "life space." He defines life space as a finite bounded region composed of the person and the various features of his perceived (physical, social and conceptual) environment. More fundamentally, the environment consists of that space outside our cocooning "life space" and it can be potentially harmful or rewarding. Lewin's findings raise several important propositions for my research on the influence of environment as a determinor of behavior. This is, perhaps, the adolescent may build a wall between himself and any harmful influence in order to achieve his goal directed behavior. In my thinking, particular adolescent nurturing settings may be used as his cocooning "walls or refuges." Thus, behavior then can be more fully determined by the contents of one's life space and the momentary interrelations within it.

Given these relationships, Lewin's ideas about regions, paths, and barriers seem useful for my purposes if we accept his notion of part-whole relationships. This view affords a context of delineating which parts of the environment are more influential in shaping the larger whole of the life space.

Thus, is provided an important connection between Lewin's (1936, 1954) theory and the way we, as environmental social scientists, go about dealing, or not dealing, with the complexities of "life space" that shape an individual's behavior. This thinking, along with how self concept emerges, in part, led me to investigate Barker's work on the use of behavioral settings.

2.6   BARKER'S THEORY OF BEHAVIORAL SETTINGS

Barker led me to examine the traditional and nontraditional community settings that adolescents use. Barker (1968) defines behavioral settings as having not only spatial but social properties that organize where certain people gather to perform particular activities at a specified time. In these settings behavior may become a function of group membership. Examples of such behavior settings are gangs, school's, clubs, sport teams, church youth activities, or other forms of community places which adolescents use. Hyram (1972) concludes that such settings may generate the deep seated values of the group which in turn may shape individual attitudes and give rise to motivations for positive behavior. Jablonsky's (1993) sociological study on a prototypical slum in Chicago after World War I shows that community behaviors can be influenced by the cultural, economic and political factors of the environment. Duneier (1992) demonstrates the significance of this concept in his sociological research on black men who patronize a community restaurant shared by college students and ghetto dwellers. His work is particularly important as it provides us with a view of how a small group of black men could use a setting as a dominant refuge. In turn, it shows that settings can afford their users security, self esteem, identity, group cohesion and connection. Another theme emerges that for black males community will be inseparably tied to the dual oppressors of racism and a society that may cast them adrift. Thus, group membership in itself for black men offers a psychic commitment and exerts for them a strong sense of control over conditions affecting their lives. These considerations augment the theory that black men's attachments are characterized by social investment and group cohesion. They also substantiate the role that black community settings serve, as a liberating force and a source of refuge. Finally, I do not believe settings are the single cause for high achievement, or that other arenas for intervention are less important. But at this stage of my research, I suspected that black adolescent's community settings represented a significant nurturing environment that could support self esteem and influence and shape the adolescent lifepath. In the next section, I more fully describe my thinking on self concept identity and the dynamics of its linkage to environment.

2.7   THEORETICAL RATIONALE

The theoretical rationale for my focus on the adolescent stage of lifepath selection came after my review of an emergent body of literature on the interconnectedness of men's life choices, adolescence, and their environment. Key to my theoretical rationale were the psychological works of Costes and Schneider (1994), Pulkkinen and Ronka (1994) and Abram and his colleagues

(1993). And, from the developmental psychology works of Nurmi (1991), Arnett (1992), Jessor (1987) and Wigfield and Eccles (1992).

- Costes and Schneider's research (1994) on self concept - indicate that, children's view of themselves is an important predictor of achievement motivation. A favorable self concept may be an important precondition for coping with difficult situations. They conclude that in turn, achievement and self concept may influence each other in a reciprocal manner.

- The level of personal control over development, identity formation, and future orientation as components for life orientation was defined by the developmental psychology research of Pulkkinen and Ronka (1994). They concluded after literature reviews and empirical findings that men's life orientation is more dependent on adaptive capabilities associated with a clear sense of identity and self percepts. They relate personal control over life and future to the individual's optimistic outlook on his personal development. Thus, future orientation which begins in adolescence is defined as a process in which the emergence of interest is followed by a period of goal setting and commitment. Positive life orientation is comprised of a clear sense of personal identity and an optimistic orientation toward the future.

- Abram and his colleagues (1993) conclude that students whose groups view difficulties as insurmountable are adversely affected by group negativity which in turn affects their self concept and need to achieve.

- In Nurmi's research (1991) on how adolescents see their future, he found that their interests are directed to their future work and education. Irrespective of their age, young men showed interest in the life events they expected to actualize at the end of their second and third decade of life. Moreover, the level of support and goals significant adults have for a child's future influences the child's future oriented interests.

- Arnett's developmental theory (1992) points out that the socialization environment either restricts or allows adolescents to act recklessly or deviate from the peer culture norm. Jessor (1987) found a correlation between the adolescents reckless behavior and that of their friends, and then made the causal interpretation that having friends who participate in reckless behavior influences and contributes to adolescent choice in reckless behavior. Thus, adolescents choose their friends on the basis of characteristics they have in common. Important for my purposes is that group dynamics define for them what behavior is acceptable and what is not.

- Wigfield and Eccles in their developmental research present a theoretical analysis on the nature and development of children's achievement choice. They conclude that early experiences of achievement can influence children's later goals.

It became necessary for me to explain these assertions in my research. Specifically, I hoped to learn how adolescent settings contribute to the experiences of black male adolescents who become adult high achievers.

2.8 CONCEPTUAL FRAMEWORK

When the dissertation was first proposed, I wanted to examine whether social capital played a role in helping black male adolescents negotiate their way out of disadvantage. Accordingly, the research draws on the belief that successful individuals learn to pursue their goals through involvements in social relationships. The concept is based on Coleman's argument that effective socialization relies in part on what happens outside the family. In my view for black male adolescents, a community of like-minded individuals is needed to expand and support their positive goal direction.

The process for black male adolescents is to become increasingly aware of the world's dimensions, reality, fantasies and possibilities through their person-environment interactional processes. And, for them, their "lifespaces" (environmental interactions) are nested in (a) self, (b) family and home, (c) the neighborhood (peers and adult influences), (d) the black community, and (e) their adolescent settings as "refuges from racism."

Accordingly, I wanted to examine how black male adolescents reared in disadvantaged black communities were prepared to obtain high achieving adult outcomes, and, what roles did settings play in their success. More importantly, how did settings accommodate the men's diversity and complexity, and their black culture, reconciling them to be more responsive to and able to cope with mainstream America.

Against this backdrop, the lives of the study participants were grounded in their high achievement which was largely determined, early on, by the presence of social capital made available to them through their experiences and relationships with others (McAdoo, 1989).

The question that framed discussion in the dissertation was: Does the presence and use of social capital by black male adolescents in controlled settings in black communities affect high achievement adult outcomes?

3 METHODS

The proposed study will use a case study methodology to examine whether high achieving black men's adolescent community places played a role in motivating their early drive to achieve. In any case, the literature indicates that black communities offer nurturing places for black children to develop healthy self concepts and self esteem which, in turn, encourages high motivation. But, there is little research specifically identifying nurturing places within black communities for black male adolescents. The research will differ from previous studies as it attempts to describe settings and the roles they played for high achieving black males, and how they were able to instill values of achievement.

3.1　RESEARCH PROCEDURE

The original research design involved an examination of three groups; an initial focus group; current community setting providers, and a core group of high achieving black men which was carried out in chronological steps as presented below. First, the study used a cross sectional self administered survey design to ascertain the high achieving black men's experiences of adolescent community places and their influence as a motivating factor for the men's chosen life path. The purpose was exploratory to help understand the interrelationship between the men's stories of community places and their desire to achieve as adults. Before conducting interviews, I identified samplings of traditional settings such as a boys' club, a team, youth center or church youth activity and had informal discussions with providers of these similar settings.
I asked them what common values they felt they instilled in young people that would motivate high achievement, and what behavioral attitudinal changes they noted in the boys, such as, leadership, self concept, or value changes. Secondly, I used focus groups as a mechanism for exploratory research to provide an opportunity to document the participants' understanding of the issues. The focus groups provided useful information for the design of the final interview schedule in which I conducted face to face interviews with individual participants at mutually agreed upon locations.

Next, I solicited a small group of high achieving black men. At the initial meeting with the group, they were asked to identify issues and recollections of their adolescent community settings. The focus group samples were divided into groups of 5 participants. One group was to be of the 35-45 year age range. The second, of the 45 - 55 year age range. These groups were to allow important opportunities to talk informally and to evaluate the different experiences of social support systems developed over the last 20-40 years and categorize the distinctions by age. Thus, I'd hoped to find that the older high achievers' resource pool was more restricted than the achievers growing up during the 70s and 80s when social programs in disadvantaged communities were plentiful. From these discussions (one session each), I explored topics to gain initial exposure to the typical experiences of the men.

Based on this approach, using the preliminary focus groups to define the variables, a semi structured interview schedule guided by a set of questions and issues to be explored was developed to assess the experiences of 30 - 40 identified high achievers. Questions included asking the participants to look back on their adolescent life and describe their perspective on what they think were the most important events or experiences in propelling them to become high achievers. The second approach addressed specific perceptual issues of their recollections of adolescent community places. For example, their interactions with the settings and the characterization of the place. Of particular importance was where the place was located and to what extent it helped determine their life path, if at all. Lastly, how did the places aid them in dealing with the stresses of their environment? Although this list is not complete, it is representative of some of the areas that I think need closer examination to address my hypotheses. Merriam (1988) concludes that this approach will afford flexibility because neither the order or exact wording of questions is predetermined.

I sought direction largely provided from other ongoing studies of black men conducted by professors, such as, A.J. Franklin at City University; Walter Stafford at NYU; and Cathy Newman at Columbia University for formulation of specific research questions.

In summary, the recruitment of participants for individual interviews began with a one page letter explaining the nature of the study and the procedures employed to ensure confidentiality and the anonymity of participants. It was distributed to an initial contact list of 150 men to select a core group of 30-40 key men for individualized interviews. A self addressed, stamped return envelope was included to facilitate the return of the questionnaire. My telephone and fax numbers were also made available within the cover letter for the potential participants to contact me. Based on this approach, an interview guide to assess the experiences of the high achieving men was developed. The guide covered both quantitative and qualitative areas. In addition to the issues identified in the focus group the guide covered demographic items and questions about each person such as age, education, income, and place of residence; current and adolescent. These variables were chosen to determine if any patterns of social support may be described according to age or location (urban, rural) of setting. Other factors to be researched addressed the men's recollections of their adolescent community places. A major objective was to describe the roles and functions of the individual settings such as: what were the social support places. . . what was the extent of their interactions with the support place. . . how were their interactions characterized . . . and where was it located? The third section was designed to explore several personality characteristics and attitudes of the men; issues of self concept, autonomy-power and the desire to think for oneself. The overall approach was based on Glaser and Strauss (1967) for the development of grounded theory.

The design of the final interview instrument explored the sociological characteristics of the men's communities of origin, the social and environmental factors that affected their lives as adolescent, The format includes yes-no multiple choice and open ended responses. It was developed based on feedback from the focus groups, and the provider interviews, and used with nearly 30 participants drawn from a list of high achieving black men who were referred by the focus group men and from referrals of the one on one participants. The criteria I had in mind for the participants identified as high achieving was tied to both economic and occupational measurement as indicated by Edwards and Polite (1992) and includes the attainment of an advanced degree, aged 35-55 years old, with an income of $50,000-100,000+ annually, and employment in a position of influence representative of various career areas. The small sample allowed for a more detailed analysis of the issues outlined in this proposal. Residency was limited to the metropolitan area for the ease of the researcher.

The directories of black professional organizations: the 100 Black Men, the Concerned Black Men, fraternal and professional associations and affiliations, NACOBA (architects), Manhattan Medical Society (doctors), and directories on judges, lawyers, real estate developers and politicians were reviewed. In addition, Morris Phillip's Guide to Black Organizations, 1987-1988 and the newly formed National Association for African Americans in Higher Education was considered to identify other potential participants. Participants did not constitute a systematic random sample but a snowball sample.

Finally the study attempted to provide an important look at how the environment influences the process of achieving in two ways. First, it showed that the black male adolescents' readiness to use positive motivating settings is established through the values instilled within him. Second, it explored the opportunities for motivation that community settings offered them.

This dissertation will attempt to pull together the relatively limited literature on black males for those who are concerned that these men, so long kept in the dark, are brought more fully into the light. A deliberate effort has been made to present as broad a range of critical variables as possible. Hopefully, the findings of this study will offer insight into the actual settings that black men used and generate further studies to confirm my expectations.

3.1.1 Research Design and Methodology

The research design consisted of a qualitative analysis of 28 high achieving black men and their recollections of the adolescent community settings that they engaged in. The indicators chosen traced the relationship of the men's adolescent experiences in settings to their high achieving adult outcomes.
The classic variables examined as measures linked their adolescent social transformations to (a) their family and neighborhood, (b) their adolescent personalities and characters, (c) the lessons they learned at their settings and (d) their recollections of how they changed after using their settings.

3.1.2 Change of Methodology

Number of interviews. Originally, 30 men were interviewed. Later, two men were dropped from the study when they failed to meet the high achievement criteria defined in the methodology. These criteria included being in possession of some or all of the factors of (a) an advanced degree, (b) income of $50,000 or more annually, and (c) employment in a position of influence.

Thus, interviewees three and six, although volunteers from one of the earlier focus groups, were dropped from the study. The study then became a group of 28 participants for analysis.

Age range. In another change, the original methodology called for study of men aged 35 to 55 years old. I suspected that this age cohort would have made it into the mainstream after gains of the civil rights movement. From the fluctuating history of social supports available in disadvantaged communities over the past 20-40 years, I hypothesized that achievers who grew up during the 60's and 70's when public sponsored recreational and esteem building projects were more readily available, would reflect more significant differences of experience than those who grew up during the early 80's. Totally unexpected were my findings that the men shared more similarity of experiences than not, no matter what age. Their stories led me to believe that most professional black men traveled a common road but their journeys were never easy. As I progressed in my research the findings revealed that each generation endured and overcame similar hardships. Thus, older men were added to the study. Six of the participants were more than 55 years old.

3.2 DESCRIPTION OF THE RESEARCH INSTRUMENTATION

3.2.1 Selecting Subjects

Focus groups. Recollections of adolescent settings were gathered from a series of men who participated in three separate focus groups. Each group consisted of 3-5 men, volunteers from a black church men's fellowship organization, who were recruited shortly after the Million Man March on Washington DC. Sessions were held as a basis of direction to prepare the interview schedule guide for individualized interviews (see Appendix 3). The men reported their recollections of the adolescent community settings they had used. Each group started off with the men completing a short bio data survey form which included asking them to list the settings they used. The survey form was followed by a series of twelve questions asked of each group over a period of one and half-hours (see Appendix 2). The men offered a wide variety of opinions regarding the relative importance of the motivational influences that they received from their settings. They also informed me of their peer friendships and the adult providers (mentors) who worked with them in their individual settings and their importance to their lives.

3.2.2 Procedure For Interviews

Individualized interviews. The research data was gathered through individualized interviews from a snowball sampling of 30 black men, adjusted to 28 men, who shared the common experience of being high achieving. I conducted face to face, one and a half to two hour interviews with men between the ages of 28-77 years old that had experienced social and economic class advancement in their journey from adolescence to adulthood.

The purpose was to provide baseline data on (a) a sample of black men who grew up in predominately segregated communities, (b) to foster the development of indicators to identify culturally specific responses among black men, and (c) to provide a basis for preventive intervention in black communities nationwide which would act as buffers and coping resources for today's black male youths. The four-page interview schedule (see Appendix 3) posed questions to gain information on the men's recollections of the adolescent community places they used.

Items from the aforementioned sections of the interview schedule were selected according to their relevance to the variables of family background and relationships, neighborhood type and influence, personality predisposition for selecting settings, setting friendships and adult and peer helpers within them, the use of settings as supports and school and work experiences.

It used a semi structured open ended format comprised of eighteen questions followed by nine short bio data survey questions which included the current living arrangement, age, income, education, profession, marital status, and more. Many of the events the men recalled from their exposure to their settings were imbued with sociological and environmental psychology significance.

Selection of the subjects was also based on theoretically determined assumptions about the characteristics of high achieving men found in the literature according to social and economic qualifications. The demographic variables used were chosen to determine if any patterns of similarity or dissimilarity could be ascribed to age group, type of neighborhood the men grew up in (segregated, integrated), or neighborhood location (urban/rural) or setting type used.

3.2.3   Participant Demographic Data

Appendix 1 summarizes the more important demographic characteristics of the men.

Age. The methodology called for a study of men ranging in age from 35-55 years old. They fell into six age groups. The majority, 11 men (39%) were middle aged and between 50-60 years old. The second group, eight men (29%) fell within the 39-49 year age range. As the study progressed and I wanted to compare historical periods of settings, I used younger men who fit in the 29-38 year old range and older men who fit within the 61-70 and then 71-77 year old ranges were added. Of these men, three men (11%) fell into the 29-38 year old range and four men, 14% fell into the 61-70 year old range. The rest, two men (7%) fell within the 71-77 year old range (See Table 1).

Profession and income. The men were evenly involved in a variety of professions that ranged from church administrators and school superintendents to lawyers, bankers, and architects (See Table 2). Their reported annual incomes showed almost a third (32%), nine men, made over $100,000 annually. Equal distributions of 18% each were found in the $60,000-$79,000 and $80,000-$99,000 ranges respectively with ten men. Eight men, 29%, made $40,000-$59,000. One man, who had a salary of $70,000, reported he had just left his position to start his own business. He estimated a new annual salary of $39,000 annually (See Table 3).

Education. Sixty one percent, 17 men, reported being college graduates. Seventy six percent of those, 13 men, had advanced degrees. The second group, 32%, nine men attended at least 2-3 years of college but reported they dropped out due to financial or personal crises. The rest 7%, two men were high school graduates (See Table 4).

Marital status. Sixty four percent, 18 men, were married with families. 25%, seven men, were single having never married. Of the rest, 11%, three men, two of them were divorced and one man was widowed (See Table 5).

Adolescent neighborhoods. The adolescent communities where the men developed, with the exception of one man, were places defined as economically disadvantaged. It is significant that 23 men, 82% came from low-income neighborhoods. Their stories told me a lot about their lives and signaled that economic hard times and the meaning of "poor" is a different definition in black communities. Also the question for me was raised about whether regional or size of community differences mattered in the black male adolescent's growing up, and did it influence the type of settings used. These differences as examined in the literature could be referred to as "environmental ecology" and in context responsible for some of the shaping of the men's lives.

The men's neighborhoods were either racially mixed urban communities (eight men) or segregated communities (20 men). The majority of the men, 14 (50%), grew up in New York City in one of the five boroughs. The second largest group, nine men (32%) grew up in the South. Two men grew up in the northeast; two men grew up in Guyana and later moved to the States in their later adolescence. One man grew up in the Midwest (See Tables 6 and 7).

3.2.4 The Challenge

In 1990 the statistics reported that one out of every four black man was incarcerated. Considering that for most inmates, jails really are crime schools, these are frightening statistics (McAdoo, 1989).

Most of the contemporary literature on black families and communities which I reviewed focused on the pathologies and deficiencies of poor blacks, and it was a condemning literature that cited their inadequacies, passivity and weaknesses. By its preoccupation with studying the behavior of the poor, the literature masked the diversity found within black communities of the four out of five black men who were not incarcerated. Moreover, it led the uninitiated reader into linking poverty with the general images of blackness. As a black woman and doctoral student raised on these "cultural deficiency" readings, I began to suspect that the social scientists' pattern of searching for pathology and "poor" blacks provided rich data for distortion.

It is also about me and how I wanted to understand what made it possible for many black men to become achievers. Based on my own experiences, I suspected that most black males who did well in school, whose parents or guardians were present and employed and who also attended church and some community support organization, were not in jail.

Also, with more study of the works of black men and women writing about the strengths of their communities and families as they grew up, I began to recognize that the answer to my research questions lay partly in describing the complexities of high achieving black men's lives. I was then inspired to ask, what made their lives different from each other and did a common thread make them the same. The study also emphasizes how these men learned to be unequal in adolescence and how they made the most of overcoming it. As I began, the themes of the dissertation tried to capture the men's perspectives of how they actually negotiated and interpreted their adolescence, and bridged the distance between their black community origins and their upper-middle class destinations.

The central characters are the 28 successful black men that I interviewed from a wide variety of adolescent environments. All had stories about their adolescence that acknowledged their lives and celebrated their accomplishments. They were generous contributors to the study and exhibited a willingness and an openness to discuss their lives in the hopes that others might benefit from their experiences.

Certainly, in assessing and understanding their journeys, it became important to me to document the effective co-ordination between their community, family, and their adolescent settings. As a consequence, I sensed that their settings evolved as not only the geographically defined places that they created but more importantly, as the emotional terrains with depth of attachments that they idealized and made unshakable in their memories. Indeed, it may be true that for many of them their settings became their reference point and the evolving dynamic memory that they constantly interpreted. In my view, it became central in the way that they made sense of and gave shape to their individual outcomes as they tried to reconcile their roots to their destinations. And, too, this dissertation is about the men's strengths and defiance against entrenched systems for failure.

4 CASE PROFILES

4.1 INTRODUCTION OF CASE PROFILES

More often than not the men's adolescent identities were challenged by the heavy hand of racism. To counteract the impact, it is my hypothesis that they needed places to buffer the negative judgements of who they were and what they could become.

Obviously, since the participants grew up in contrasting communities and times, and used different settings, I needed to understand what were the textures within their families, communities, and themselves that led to their central tendencies of survival seen from one generation to the next.

What follows is a sampling of the 28 participants through presentation of eight men profiled who grew up in six contrasting neighborhood types: (a) northern urban, racially mixed; (b) southern urban, racially mixed; (c) northern urban segegated; (d) southern urban segregated; (e) northern small town, racially mixed, and (f) southern small town, segregated.

The men varied in professions and ages. There is JHS, the 29 year-old Chief of Staff for a powerful legislator; BA, 45, the chief electrical engineer for a major urban city agency, JC, a 51 year-old psychologist, and TC, the 28 year-old Legislative Director for a city councilman. Then there is CM, 49, a successful real estate developer, JH, the 56 year-old high level administrator for a Human Services Agency, KP, the 54 year old lawyer, and college professor; and RJ, 72, the retired administrator for a state redevelopment agency.

The next pages will have each man presented in a brief manner to characterize the life histories and stories of all the men. It intends to give the reader a sense of the participants, as well as highlight those areas of their lives that illustrate how early activities, settings, and circumstances were able to contribute to the men's early motivations for high achievement.

4.1.1 Case Profile #1

Introductory remarks. JHS reflects the younger men of the study and those who grew up in northern urban racially mixed neighborhood types. Raised in a single parent family, his adolescent setting was his after school ROTC program where he gained a sense of adulthood, discipline, character, and heightened aspirations. He shows us how gaining the critical survival strategies of interpersonal power, and affiliating with others were acquired by the men in their settings.

JHS. JHS is 29, tall and thin with a boyish face that belies his razor sharp mind, carriage, and his determination. He is personable, ruthless, and the Chief of Staff for one of the state's senates most powerful members. We settle in his office at the end of his long day of soothing constituents.

He was born in New York City and raised in the black community of Harlem in the early 80's. After his mother became too ill to care for him when he was 13 years old, he moved with his maternal aunt and cousin in a racially mixed neighborhood into a tenement.

His early memories of the neighborhood he lived in were its transition from a predominately Jewish community to a Dominican and black community. Each of the three cultures remained and lived in what he called their "dividing lines," where the level of service delivery was always different. He lived in the last remaining Jewish cluster. When he spoke of it, he paused and furrowed his brow and said, "when I looked at the different incomes of the communities, it was like the tale of two cities, and I grew up learning that." JHS seemed poised on the boundary line of two distinct realities, race and class. He examined his choice to befriend and play with black kids who lived adjacent to his neighborhood and in the projects of his old neighborhood in Harlem. When I asked him why he responded, "I wasn't satisfied with my community. I liked the time I lived in Harlem but my mother didn't necessarily want me to live in Harlem with other blacks," he explained. "She was very resentful towards the community for a lot of reasons. I had no desire to live with white people. I was not hostile to Hispanics. I just thought that black people should be with black people and white with white and Hispanic with Hispanic. That's how I came up. I was interested in learning about my people." I suspected his adolescent wanderings took the form of his determined pursuit.

It became immediately clear that he had two sets of friends, those from the community and those from his former neighborhood. Both sets played basketball with him on the community courts in playgrounds or parks, and developed a camaraderie with him where he recalled they "talked about basketball, girls, and life." A big grin spread over his face as he reported that he and his neighborhood friends spent many hours talking and laughing until late at night.

When JHS was ready for high school his choice reflected his strong views on being with his own people. His mother's choice for him was the United Nations International School. Instead, he selected a black and Latino high school in the adjacent community and stated, "I felt it important to be around black people. I just had this profound dislike of white people." His viewpoint he commented was based on his studies of the Civil Rights Movement and his friendship with the father of one of his friends from his old community. Being fatherless, he offered this observation, "The man became an adult male role model for me. He would always sort of pick on me and ask me what did your parents teach you about school, the community, being black?" Basically after

JHS had no answer, the man informed him he had to learn. I suspect those times were the turning point of his life as the man and his son began JHS' education about the black community and his black culture. "They took me around Harlem and talked about black history until the wee hours of the morning and showed me where Malcolm X spoke or Congressman Powell started his boycott. JHS said with a sense of admiration, "His point was that this is where the folks lived and you should understand that and know that whatever you do, you can't get away from the folks no matter what your mother raises you as 'cause this is where you have to be." The man, JHS clarified, showed him that he could achieve and leave Harlem but that he should never leave his black skin. Instead, he could be proud of it as he achieved. I was certain that for JHS, the man validated his feeling that his racial identity was important and not limiting as he defined himself.

  At the center of his life was his mother. I suspected that much of his determination to achieve could be attributed to her. He described her as a single parent to him, her only child. She had been a teacher and then became a social worker. He leaned back in his chair, softly smiled and said, "Mother had been at Bennett College and back then it was like Spellman. She used to say it was a lot better. I would say she was very bourgeois and very structured which I really resented. It was ingrained in her, trained in her, and she wanted me to be that way." He remembered it was his mother who pushed him to learn as much as he could and go as far as he could academically. Early on, she would take hi to the library every afternoon after school and sit with him while he did his homework while, he lamented, his friends were playing and hanging out. While there, his mother questioned him about his homework and guided him along the middle class path. He sighed, "I began to look at those books and tried to figure out what I wanted to do with the rest of my life." His mother was very respectful of institutions and especially government and hoped he would become a lawyer one day. The other woman in his life was his maternal aunt whom he lived with. She gave him additional direction. "At 13, I went to live with my aunt and her son, who was two years older than me and in a lot of ways since I had no brother or sisters, filled the role of a brother," he said. He remembered the definite tension between the cousins because "he (his cousin) felt he would have got twice as much if I wasn't there." His aunt was a telephone operator in a hospital. She gave him everything, which caused some resentment from her son, and JHS' memories of her were warm. He had a good relationship with his aunt saying, "My aunt was more practical than my mother because she could understand my arguments on various points, such as black communities or associations and the like. She and I had an interesting relationship because I was always challenging her. We used to argue a lot because I was so outspoken but it was constructive. My cousin wasn't like that; he would just go into his room and not say anything for a day." His aunt had a great respect for the church and went every Sunday with him, which he hated. He paused and said, "It was ridiculous, old people sitting in church that they had been going to since childhood, listening to the same recycled sermon." He thought it was a total waste and questioned the logic of it. But his aunt made him go and even become involved with the church's youth activities. He reasoned it was because she wanted him to be a normal kid. JHS saw himself as rebellious and clarified, "I didn't listen to anybody. I guess I was rebelling against myself and those who tried to control me, like mother and my aunt." He didn't trust adults especially telling me, "I was not an accepting person, and I liked to argue about the logic of everything all the time." In school he was in the honors program and took advanced courses where even then, he was ahead of his class. In his senior year, he decided to stop school and "hang out" after he determined that his teachers weren't "qualified" educators. In other words, he said, "I used to talk to them like I talked to my friends." He stopped for a few weeks until a black woman teacher guided him back to school after she asked him, "Why are you going to be like the rest of these kids?" He said, "I then took inventory of myself and I knew that in some way I was rebelling because mother never let me go out like other kids my age. Later, I became worried that I might not be able to graduate."

His recollection of the adolescent groups he participated in included the places of his church youth activities and his informal basketball teams. But the one he saw as the most significance was his ROTC affiliation at his black and Latino high school. I was surprised since he made a point of rebelling against anyone who tried to control him. But he said the prime reason he joined was because it was different; "It was sort of a click, a club, and a lot of people became my friends." He learned to enjoy the group marches, and military discipline and that a real army officer was assigned to lead them. He liked the experience of learning from someone who was formally educated but also rose from the ranks to become an officer. Another draw, he explained, was that the boys took a lot of trips in and out of state, spent time on aircraft carriers, and went to mini boot camp. He found those activities attractive. When I asked him for more clarity on the setting's attraction, he explained in this way, "I think throughout I had a desire to have a click. Not having any brothers or sisters, and my cousin and I not really being that close, and with totally different personalities, I needed other people." The boys who attended the ROTC were black and Latino kids from all over the city and from his classes at school. For JHS, the distinction of his organization was that it offered an educational opportunity and travel. Most of the boys who joined had less stable families than he. "Some students," he said, "ran away from home a lot, and stayed with other students. I mean it was like a family there. We helped each other and the older boys advised the younger ones because many of the kids came from unstable families and couldn't talk to their parents." Surprisingly, racism was even found in his refuge as he recalled, "We had one naval instructor who bordered on being a constructive racist, he openly said to us he never really dealt with black kids before. He didn't need to say a lot more." But the other instructors treated the boys, as he said "like they were one of the guys," talked to them as equals and were approachable. For a lot of the kids, JHS felt the setting gave them a sense of adulthood and built character. He spent several years in the ROTC and articulated the impact by telling me that he saw it as one of the most defining experiences of his youth. "When you got there, it was the networking that really woke me up to know that you could do things that you may want to do, if you really focused."

I suspected as we ended the interview that he still saw life that way. He certainly used the lessons of his ROTC experience when after high school he became involved with student government in college. It was there that he became a key negotiator for student rights against the school administration. From there he went on to become a national student rights negotiator which led him to local New York City politics. Further networking with old college contacts led him to his current job.

Interviewer's observation. There are four main themes in JHS' adolescent life. First is his community where he learns to resent its distinct boundaries of race and class, and he searches for his black identity with blacks like himself. Second, is his family and a mother who encourages high achievement. Third, is his personality that is precocious, angry and rebellious which allowed him to excel but left him unanchored and seeking. But it was his setting that provided him with the structure he needed to guide his competitiveness and gave him the companionship, adult, and peer interactions he needed to move forward.

4.1.2 Case Profile #2

Introductory remarks. Like JHS, BA too grew up in a single parent household in a northern urban racially mixed neighborhood type with distinct boundaries. Nearly 15 years older than JHS, his setting was a community PAL sports team where he found adult male role models and learned to be a team player. He is an example of how positive nurturing counteracted the dilemmas of his adolescent family and community.

BA. BA is a 45 year-old man of medium brown complexion with close-cropped hair that is receding. He is relatively short (about 5'6") and heavy set but his carriage and confident demeanor make him seem taller. He is an engaging, talkative man who works as the chief electrical engineer for a city agency. Part of his interest in participating in this project had to do with creating an opportunity for him to revisit his roots and spin the tales of his struggles growing up.

BA was born in Puerto Rico. After his fifth birthday, home became the integrated, ethnically diverse community he grew up in within one of this country's major northern cities. He explained, "My community was very funny because each avenue represented a different ethnic group -- white, black, Hispanic, Irish, and Italian -- which was very strange, but had a little bit of everything." He recalled a community that was, in part, a ghetto with gangs, fights, drugs, and murders. In another, wooded areas where students from a major Ivy League university studied and, says he, "white folks walked around in streets more open and with more light than a city park." From a very young age, BA bitterly lamented, "I had seen people right in front of me shooting up drugs in the stairway . . . . I had seen people jump off the roof, or get hit by a car, and if two kids started to fight and grown-ups came around, they'd start betting on a winner, so you had to get the thing done because you were scared out of your wits. I did and saw all those things but I was strong and I didn't let them affect me." When he was 13 years old, he delivered dry cleaning in the white part of the community, a job his friend got him. This experience opened his eyes. He said, "It was almost like it was another world besides my own. There were things I saw that I liked that I would never be able to afford, a world which held promise and where I was just a visitor. BA grinned and added, "I kind of accepted that as my new norm that Donna Reed was out there, and there was really nobody for me. In my world, I didn't have to do anything; I just had to be there. So, it (his job at the dry cleaners) showed me a lot of interesting new things."

Within his own community BA found some refuge with his own network of sports activities, friends, and school. And, through his mother's efforts, in which she insisted that he go to church "and things like that," he joined a community Catholic Charity Big Brother organization. Because, he said, "She tried to help me for the simple fact that I wasn't into drugs or anything like that and because I lived in a house with no male influence." I sensed the cruel imprint of his school life when he talked about his white teachers in his neighborhood school. There was Mrs. C, he said, "I was like her pet. She had a male and female pet. I was the male pet. I wanted to be good so Mrs. C would be glad." Another teacher, his math teacher, Mr. R, told him, "Find something in life you can do with your hands because if you go into clerical work you will be blacklisted." He didn't fare any better with his first black teacher, Mr. D. As BA explained, "He had this rod and if we did anything bad, he took us into the closet and gave us a good whack. That was not allowed during the time yet, he did it, and we were pretty straight kids." It was in the later years of his high school experience that one teacher changed his lifepath when he asked BA what he wanted to do after graduation. BA couldn't answer. The teacher told him he would be a good electrician and BA said, "Fine." He was sent to a vocational high school specializing in the skills he needed and BA said he and his classmates felt they were special. "It was really fun there," he said, "everybody had a secret goal but they didn't want to show or tell anybody that they cared because you were supposed to be bad. Not bad as a gangster or anything because there were kids there that were into gangs and robbing and stuff like that. Many of us weren't into that, but we didn't want to show ourselves as soft or that we listened to our mothers." The way he survived, he emphasized was through the close contact he developed with a circle of classmates, whom he felt, were smarter than he was, and also sports oriented. After high school, BA enrolled in college and attended for three years with hopes of becoming a physical education teacher. Getting out of the ghetto, he wanted me to know, was carefully planned.

    BA's family, his mother and two elder sisters, lived in a rundown tenement in the ghetto. His mother moved to the ghetto after she divorced his father and left Puerto Rico. He described his mother as a light-skinned Puerto Rican, single mother who struggled to raise her children. They were very poor and subsisted on public assistance in a rat and roach infested apartment. As the only male in the family, BA supplemented the family income working odd jobs as a delivery boy. When he described his sisters, he smiled saying, "they were older, nice looking, brown skinned teenagers who joined one of the gangs." BA measured his troubled relationship with his sisters as loving but conflicted. He explained, "My sisters got black eyes from me because they were hanging out in the streets and I was still anchored to home, sports, TV, and Donna Reed. I was basically learning American ways from TV and it was funny because I never saw anybody on it like me. It was like if you looked up at the sky and saw a million stars, none of them looked like me." Distressed, he would go up on the roof of his tenement and look at the stars and reflect on the harsh realities of his life. His voice was thick with emotion when he described the lifestyle of the women in his family. "My sisters and mother were out there. They were all party girls. Mother used to go dancing, she was "a back seat person" who dyed her brown hair blonde and had many male friends. I was very possessive of my mother and sisters and I didn't like anybody that came to the house for their little parties. They used to fight with me to try to get their space. "It was three against one."
I learned that BA's father, a dark skinned black man, had remained in Puerto Rico after refusing to join his wife in the States. BA remembered seeing him seven years later when he was 13 years old. He said, "He wanted to take me back to Puerto Rico with him and put me through college because I was doing pretty well in school. One of his requirements was that I never saw my mother again, and I

didn't like that. I rebelled against him whenever he came to visit." I sensed his distress, but asked him to continue. "My father was a playboy, a lover boy, and I was never close to him. I was bitter," he said, "then and now." "I promised myself that I would never be like him. I didn't want a broken home. I didn't want my children to grow up without a father. In a sense he helped me with that because my hatred of him made me the husband and father that I am today." His mind then moved on to his maternal cousins who often visited the household. "They all belonged in gangs. In some respects, I withdrew from their world with my greatest fear being to become like them. Maybe being a boy it was easier than being a girl. So I roamed and did almost what I wanted to." From his painful recollections I sensed that BA's personal liberation from his family was tied up with the survival of his adolescent goal to become different than they.

From a very young age, work was central to him. As an adolescent he had worked holding down an assortment of delivery boy jobs and he knew the value of hard work. He described himself as a loner who made friendships carefully and only with boys as ambitious as he. He was a good kid and enjoyed all his friends but was unable to keep his opinions to himself. He was more rambunctious than they, bigger and physically stronger, which he attributed to the "welfare food." He was always willing to take chances and fearful of nothing. He was certainly smart enough. After a long silence, he seemed to be thinking out loud, then said, "I remember one day crying after my mother's family told me the whole story about my father. Of course it was against him. They told me that since I was black like he, the only livelihood that would be open to me in this country was to be a pimp because that was what black people did. I didn't want to be bad and I cried like a baby. I couldn't understand why that was the only road open to me. I questioned whether they were correct." BA added, "I think that it was that uncertainty that made me determined to master the skills to make them incorrect."

I asked him about the adolescent places he valued and used in his community. He named the church, which his mother sent him to. From it he attended the Catholic Big Brother program which had organized football and baseball teams supervised by off-duty cops. BA believed the teams were an escape from his reality. "When I was on the team, there was no home. There was no Puerto Rico, black or white. There were no gangsters. There was only a team and you became one with each other." He added, "When I was on the field or court, I wasn't in the ghetto." He took everything the team gave him and it gave him a place to hit hard and release his anger and frustration. "I let out a lot of stuff. It showed me organization. It showed me respect. It showed me that I had to work hard. It saved me." In contrast, BA recognized that he had restrictions at home, sisters with moods and other "stuff". He admitted he never brought a friend to his home. Perhaps so, but he was allowed to stay outside until 11 o'clock at night until he was 16, after that, even later. The teams' coaches were off-duty cops with families of their own. BA's favorite coach, a black cop, worked him hard, cheered for him when he won, and showed him how to work harder. "I would hear his voice from the sidelines telling me to get up if I got hit hard -- 'get up -- the game is not over -- you haven't won yet' and that was enough," he said. As I listened to BA, I came to understand his shared experience of searching for support in his adolescent life like the other men of the study. Being a team member broke new ground for him and he linked his success as an adult to his experiences on the sports teams. He said, "I learned early on that since I was one of the main players, they needed me to jell. In a sense, it made me have to relate with my teammates who were black, white, Irish, Italian, and Hispanic. I learned about them and about their worlds. Paddy was the Irish quarterback. Donald was the black strong defensive. We had to come together every week during the team meetings and figure out how we were going to beat the next team. All those people were in my football and basketball world and it was the only world for me."

Interviewer's observation. In the end, I concluded that BA's "protected world" of sports kept him off the streets, drug free, and gang free. I came to understand that BA's bonding with his teammates came on the heels of his conscious decision to overcome the desperation of his family life and community. Citing their inadequacies, I came to understand something fundamental about each of them. In his eyes, his mother's lasting contribution was her lifestyle, which he rejected, but of equal importance was her role in directing him to the church team as a refuge away from both the streets and his family. His community offered an uncertain future, which heightened his efforts to escape. His self directed middle class values provided him with the central insights necessary to do what he needed to do to move forward.

4.1.3 Case Profile #3

Introductory remarks. JC reflects men who grew up in two parent families in southern urban racially mixed neighborhoods. His setting was his high school basketball team. He illustrates how the men learned to make things work in "the power structure" and honed their determination to win."

JC. JC, 51, is a psychologist and the head of his own consulting firm. He is a tall, well built light-skinned black man with short graying hair.
The interview was conducted in my living room one summer evening. Our session felt easy and enjoyable.

JC spent his adolescence in a large southern metropolis in an interracial neighborhood during the late 50's. When he was 14 years old, the family, his parents and younger sister and brother, moved to the community from a protected black enclave in a small southern town. He described the startling differences of the two environments in this way. "In my earlier town, we were almost like a community as I look back. It was like a protected enclave. We did all right; there weren't many of us in the neighborhood, maybe three or four families of color, and we were surrounded by white people. So, we had to get along. The theory then was violence against blacks. We weren't violent. But we were trained to be violent and taught to be together if we had to protect ourselves. So, we blacks were close." The family lived in his mother's old neighborhood. Her cousin was the minister of the church, and all the people there, he learned, were relatives somehow. He said they never knew any fear because the men had weapons to protect themselves and the women knew how to do things. And families built their own houses with their own hands. He went on to describe the town as a core of people and relatives of his mother's who were mostly professionals or teachers such as his parents. "From them," he said, "I learned early on because we knew them (the teachers) since we were small. When I got to school they were the same people, so naturally, I got all the breaks and understood how the game was played.

When I moved to the larger city of Baltimore, I was just stupefied." I sensed that the transition for him was painful as he explained, "I was taller, could play ball better, and I was smart like the white kids and I had been used to grown people, not kids. And, it was interesting that some of the white teachers couldn't stand it (his presentation). They just couldn't understand how a Negro boy could do this and be from the south too. He leaned forward and thoughtfully said, "they were real smart teachers too, but they never would look at a black kid."

He remembered his neighborhood as a transition too. "Like most black people that move to the city it was like moving into a neighborhood that white people had moved out of. So it was in transition," he said. He paused and I found the moments of silence and reluctance were important to the story. "The white kids that were there, did not play with us. The black kids there were totally different than in his earlier neighborhood and my life with them revolved basically around playing ball." In getting further clarification he added, "Before, I had lived in an upper middle class black neighborhood, but my new neighborhood was racially mixed and middle class. And, too, the black basketball players I hung out with in the neighborhood were from a lower class. So I was kind of hanging out with the wrong crowd to be a middle class boy." From him I learned that the town offered few social activities for black youths except for school and sports. He clarified it and said, "We really didn't do that much, we didn't go to the movies. We didn't have Jack and Jill (a black society association) so, it was basically school and basketball." I learned he became a part of sports groups. He articulated the distinction between the towns in this way, "I was pretty much on my own. I didn't have any people, no family or relatives besides my immediate family. I just had the basketball teams. He recalled the team's self sufficiency and collaboration and said, "they (the black team) would play real hard and they didn't want to lose. But it wasn't the thing where you would go home with everybody; there were a few people you couldn't go to visit at home."

Mention of his teachers took him back to his integrated all male school. He struggled to understand them and their impact on him and then described them in this way. "I was probably more mature than the teachers. I had a gift for keeping my head under pressure. In high school, that's all you need to win. But there was a total disrespect, even though I was smart, they wouldn't, they couldn't believe it (that he was smart), and when they found out they made a mascot of me. So, I was the exceptional kind of kid. And, it was so interesting." JC believed his experiences in both his communities taught him how to make things work with the power structure. And he said, "I was a hard worker. I didn't lose. I would stay in something; I was determined. And when I put my mind to something, I did it. There was no question of not doing it. It was just how long it was going to take and when was I going to get it done."

JC identified his family life as his source of inspiration. He was the oldest of the three children and his family lived in private houses in both communities. He took the family inventory and began by describing his parents. They were teachers with his father a college math teacher and his mother a high school home economics teacher. JC proudly informed me that his father, who also owned a real estate business, was the first person of color to have a real estate license in the state.

His father, born less affluent than his wife, was raised as an orphan. His family members were mostly illiterate. But he was determined, hardworking, and smart. JC smiled softly as he remembered watching his father spend his life trying to impress his wife and her family. Within his community, he worked very hard to compete with what JC called the class difference. JC's mother was a light skinned black woman from a more upper class family. Her parents had inherited a part of the plantation their ancestors had been slaves on. So, JC said, his grandparents had been rich when they moved to Virginia, which he said explained their attitude. His mother had been a top student in college and in his growing up years, she was an avid reader. She taught her children not only how to do things to take care of themselves, such as sew, cook, and iron but also the social graces. He said, "Such as, to eat dinner at the table, make conversation, and have good manners." She also taught him how to be involved in his community and he remembered volunteering for local charity work that his parents participated in.

JC's maternal grandmother, whom he lived with for a short time until his parents graduated from college, lived across the street and she made sure that the children got their religious upbringing. She doted on JC, the oldest of the grandchildren. In terms of family, whatever the impulse, he saw a closeness, which made up the protective enclave he referred to as he matured. It also provided for him, I came to understand from our conversation, his models for hard work, the distinctions of class, and the ability for upward mobility through education.

Mention of his adolescence led JC to identify himself as "industrious, smarter than he was supposed to be and into paper and stuff." He clarified and added, "Because that's the way my father insisted we be." JC was an honor role student and he remembered being able to focus things for the group because he had a gift for being cool under pressure. He called it one of his roles in his school, which was just turning predominately black.

When I asked him to tell me about the places he used as an adolescent, he named many but it was his school basketball team that he said had the most impact. It was there that he became the captain of the team and leader of his school marching band. The band, he said, taught him teamwork, and thinking things through. There was also the practicing and then the performance. All, which he believed, led to teaching him the exercise of learning and how to persevere.

But basketball at school and informally on his neighborhood basketball team was most valued by him. He felt that life in his neighborhood mostly revolved around playing basketball because there were no other outlets. He said, "I would play every afternoon from sun up to sun down. We played against some men in the playground. I mean it was violent because they would be frustrated from working so, they would play hard and they didn't want to lose. It was good training." In high school JC continued to play ball. As the "star" of his mostly white team, he went on to become the team captain and lead them to a championship season. The team beat both all white and black schools. I suspected that it was his way of controlling his environment. His response was, "I remember I was always the liaison with the power. The one able to make things work with the power structure. I was never the biggest, nor the fastest, nor the best at anything. But I could always get the group to focus and our relationships were good. We never really got into any real disagreements." While he may have joined the team as the only recourse for recreational activity, he concluded that basketball was very instrumental for him in teaching him how to deal with life issues like many of the people in his community and his parents did. It prepared him, he said, to compete with himself and best his own records. And, he added, his college career was as a result of a basketball scholarship orchestrated by his white coach. But it was the basketball team (at school) that helped him. He learned to get along in an integrated situation with teammates, to be a team member, and to think things through together. At the same moment he commented, "You learned the difference between practice as a good exercise and the actual doing of the job." He connected it this way. "You always practiced much better than you would have to perform. In the performance you had the uniform and stuff, so you could make mistakes and cover it up. So I learned some little lessons in there."

Interviewer's observation. JC's life was directed by four aspects of his experiences. First is his community where he experienced the difference between a small and caring segregated southern community and an urban and divided southern neighborhood. Second, is his family that was solidly middle class and instilled in him his social and intellectual values. Third, was JC himself who inwardly realized that he must win at whatever cost to prove his worthiness for the race. Last, was his setting where he excelled as team captain but learned the basic principles of the difference between surface achievement versus having true substance which carried him throughout his adult life.

4.1.4   Case Profile #4

Introductory remarks. Another of the younger men was TC, who like JHS, grew up in a northern urban neighborhood. But it was in the black community of Harlem. Like JHS, he did not live with his mother but instead was raised by loving grandparents. His setting was the community Boy Scouts where he learned discipline, competition, and the tasks required to achieve a goal. He is a good example of the process the men went through to develop and reconcile their identities.

TC. TC is 28 years old. Tall, broad shouldered and of medium brown color with short curly black hair. He is classically handsome with a keen intelligence and a ready smile. He works as the Legislative Director for one of New York City's most powerful councilmen. As we sat in my living room one evening, he leaned back and began to tell his story.

Although born in St. Croix, like KP, TC grew up in a tight knit segregated black community that was located within a larger community. Unlike KP, TC's community was urban and he grew up during the late 80's in a public housing project. He remembered his community, Harlem, as a place where blacks had a tremendous connection that kept them together. He defined it as their mutual, forced plight of racism, low wages, and the inability to find affordable housing in other parts of the city. TC described his neighborhood as a place of tremendous fun in his adolescence and called it an "adventure playland" which offered him and his peers a core of good friends, adults, and family members to care about them and a variety of places where they could have fun. His core of neighborhood "best friends," he recalled, "sat together with him in school, called him every day after school and stayed on the phone for hours, and went everywhere with him." As he painted his comforting images of growing up, he clarified that his adolescence occurred in a time before crack and extreme violence in the community. He added that then, the worse disadvantage was the neighborhood bully and the gangs that existed only recruited older boys, 17, 18, and 19. When they had fights, their encounters never led to fatalities as seen later in the decade.

As an honors student, he attended classes out of his community with several of his best friends, who like he, were gifted. He remembered his teachers as knowledgeable but admitted he hated many of them for the way they labeled him because of his race. I sensed the frustrations that he and his friends endured from the silences between his reflections. In response to their treatment, he said, he and his friends took great glee in being mischievous, class cut ups, and clowns. He smiled and added that once, when a teacher challenged the boys to get out if they didn't want to be in school, ". . . we stood up looked at each other and left . . ." Undoubtedly, the boys were affected by the painful undercurrents of racism in the school and doubts about their place in that world. However, like KP, the rejections did not dissuade TC and he excelled academically as he explained, "I always did my homework and knew the answers to the teachers' questions, but my acts were at times more a defense mechanism than anything else."

Within his community was TC's family.

He was the only child of his single mother but when he was six years old, he was sent to live with his maternal grandparents in the States. His relationship with his father and mother thereafter was a puzzle, as he never mentioned them again in connection to his life's journey. TC's grandparents raised him in the Harlem community. And he and his grandfather, a retired carpenter and his grandmother, a retired maid, lived as a family. He beamed when he described his grandparents whom he called "his constants," and added, "as close to me as I was to them." In his early years, his grandfather became his daily companion while TC attended the daycare where his grandfather was the president of the senior citizen center. TC remembered his grandparents had deep roots in the housing complex community and a wide circle of friends and neighbors who supported and looked out for one another. Each day TC, his grandmother, and his grandfather's friends would sit in the housing complex recreation area and talk and play checkers. Looking back, TC credits those times with his grandfather and his friends as teaching him how to be patient and enduring. On Sunday afternoons, TC's uncles would visit and he, his grandparents, and the men of the family would sit and talk among themselves. He is still awed as he spoke of those times; then commented, "they would sit and enlist my views on current events and the political situation and really listen to me. . . and quiz me on history and ask me. . . what did Napoleon conquer and why, or. . . what did you learn in school?" Then they would tell him funny stories and teach him, as he called it, life's lessons. The depth of his love for his grandmother shines through when he describes her. I also learned that several years ago he moved back in with her to look out for her after his grandfather passed away. She is described as the family disciplinarian when he was bad, but she was also the main person responsible for keeping the family stable and success directed. Interchangeably, I sensed that TC seemed both burdened and inspired by growing up in a mainly adult world. But, too, like KP, he appreciated having been supported and motivated by a family that gave him love, and tried to direct his commitment and purpose.

Like KP, TC described himself as an academic achiever, a gifted honors student who was highly competitive as an adolescent. The dichotomy of his personality seemed that although he liked to kid and clown a lot, he also had another more serious, thoughtful side. He revealed it as his genuine interest in helping peers within his community who were less achievement oriented than he. A math whiz, when he was sixteen, he volunteered to be a peer counselor and assisted kids struggling with their academics. He described that experience as one of his more rewarding which instilled in him an early ambition to become involved in the Harlem community at some level to benefit those less fortunate than he.

When I asked TC about the places within the community he used, he remembered the informal sports teams and playing with friends but the place he considered as most impacting on his life was his involvement in the Boy Scouts. TC attended Scouts from age 13-17 and even became a master scout. He joined, he said, not so much because he was drawn to the organization's rituals but because he grew up in a mainly adult world and he wanted to make friends and master some of the skills the scouts taught such as hiking, camping, and swimming. As scouts, he and his best friends from the neighborhood and four other neighborhood boys met weekly. His scoutmaster lived across the street. He remembered coming from an environment of adults, to an exposure to other boys and their ideas. He enjoyed learning how to develop for the first time, his interpersonal human skills of interacting with other boys and forming friendships. Equally important were his first experiences of independence and freedom on his own. And, he learned that new experiences and survival skills required developing specific knowledge, focus, and competitiveness. TC learned from his scouts' experience that part of growing up was to be able to work within a group instead of as an individual. He learned to love the challenge of discipline and competition to achieve his goals and recognized that goals were achieved by doing every task he had to do right. An important insight that he raised was one of his reflections comparing his grandparents and the scouts. Like most black parents, he told me that they wanted to instill in him discipline and self control to help him survive the obstacles and rejections he would encounter from the outside world. But, he explained, because of the circumstances of their own lives, racism, poverty, and other life problems, they had trouble achieving it for themselves. He went on to clarify and added, ". . . black parents (they) don't know how to instill discipline and they don't know how to discipline. . . you can't instill discipline and self control. . . it has to be taught in a well thought out and applied manner. . .." For TC, the scouts were able to succeed in instilling control and discipline in him by teaching him how to use it through the intricate tasks the boys were assigned, and expected to complete correctly. He saw the ability to apply discipline and self-control in any situation as one of the most formative factors in his growing up.

He went on to build a rich and varied life by applying himself with vigor in school, friendships, and everything he did. As we ended the interview, I asked him if he had any final thoughts on his adolescent years. He said, . . . I think I had unique opportunities that were helpful in shaping my experiences and how I felt about myself which were able to open up other opportunities throughout my life."

Interviewer's observation. TC gained rich experience from his community through his exposure to his grandparents, relatives, and the friends and neighbors of his Harlem community. He realized that hard work, education, and learning were the norms. His family fully supported him, encouraged his learning and gave him much love. His academic life outside his community exposed him to racism and the inequalities of life for blacks. His personality and his ability to turn adversity to levity was useful. But it was his feeling that all the aspects of his life came together when the boy scouts taught him the disciplines and survival skills required to develop the specific knowledge, focus, and competitiveness he needed to achieve. That boy scouts also offered friendship and fun for him was also important.

4.1.5 Case Profile #5

Introductory remarks. CM was one of the men raised in the pre-civil rights south in a southern urban segregated neighborhood. Calling himself an underachiever during his adolescence, he shows how he turned that bitterness into achievement in his later years. He credited his Boy Scout experience as influential because it exposed him to an expanded world, and how to treat others, and gave him certain moralities and aspirations he felt were
not taught at home. He is one of the men who felt defeated from the harshness of growing up in an unequal environment but realized he could overcome it in time.

CM. CM, 49 is a successful real estate developer. He is dark skinned, tall, and brawny with a barrel chest. His voice is deep and rumbling and his tone is quite curt but when he smiles his face lights up. Our interview was conducted in the living room of his father-in-law's house during the family's regular Sunday afternoon visit. His wife, her grown siblings, and their families and his father-in-law sat visiting in the adjoining room while we talked to give CM the privacy he requested.

CM grew up in a southern urban segregated city during the early sixties. The city, Baton Rouge, Louisiana was fairly large, he remembered, and "truly segregated." "I grew up in the old school," he said "under the black plight that brought blacks up to say, yes sir, no sir to the white man. In fact, my mother would discipline me if I didn't show whites respect." CM and his family lived in a rented house in the town's black community. "Most of the town's blacks worked as household servants or support staff for whites." "It was rare to find a black professional. It was just hard times," he commented. "blacks were unemployed a lot. They shined shoes and they sold things on the street. Any way to make a buck and from having to steal something to support their families." He paused, and seemed to be lost in his memories of that time. The he furrowed his brow and I suspect he found those memories still painful. He spoke again, "Although there was a lot of good there, there was too much negative stuff going on. Too much to mention in this interview. I couldn't wait to leave and go somewhere else. I had to get away from there with the expectations I had internally."

As we talked further, it became clear to me that his black school offered him some support. He smiled softly when he spoke of his high school teachers. "I used to live right next door to one of my teachers, and she was instrumental in teaching me because she taught me through all the grades. I had the fear of her in my heart because she didn't play and I also used to work with her husband doing odd jobs. So, I got good grades in her class." Another supporter was his high school band teacher who was a friend of his uncle. CM admired the man he explained, "You could tell good people from bad people. He saw the need to pull me off to the side and give me hands on instruction. I did better with one on one training because it was difficult for me to learn in a large group and be competitive."

But, he admitted, he also had outside influences attacking him too. When he turned 18 and was in his senior year of high school, like JHS, who attended a northern segregated school, CM decided to quit school and play hooky. Unlike JHS, who found his teachers unqualified to teach him, CM left, he said, because "I had never been the kind of person that could fit in with the norm. I wasn't a good student and my attention span wasn't like it should be. I was getting older and I felt the need to be an individual. I couldn't get interested any further in school because I didn't have anyone to support me to go to school."

Whatever the impulse, he joined a neighborhood gang. His black community had various neighborhood gangs and turf disputes, he commented and, "There were a lot of shootings and a lot of violence and stuff there such as drinking, quitting school, and hanging out. All this negative stuff was there. I guess if there is bad luck, you have to have some good luck." He shook his head slowly, smiled, and responded, I guess luck had to happen to me to survive some of that stuff." He joined the gang, he said, because during those days blacks had gangs and there would be disputes about turf, and going to this movie or that school and that type of thing, which appealed to him. "It looked like they were going somewhere," he said, "and I wanted to find out. Nobody knew I was a thug for the longest. For a few years I learned how to shoot craps, win a few dollars, and learned to curse. It was just a part of being mischievous."

Later he offered this observation, "I was the kind of guy that could go both ways. I had friends that were good whom I considered had potential. One friend turned out to be a minister. To me, he looked like he was going someplace, and I wanted to find out how, but I thought it was taking him too long because he had to do this and that. I would say, shoot some dice and hope to win a million quick, he added.

CM stayed in his town until "Uncle Sam" called him. "It was then," he said, "I felt if I could get away from there (his hometown) and into a different environment (the army) where nobody knew me, I could reappear as the person I wanted to be, get into school and have aspirations." In the service he eventually got his GED. After service, he went to college under the GI bill. By that time, his determined pursuit of aspiring was tied to becoming educated. "It was then I really enjoyed going to school," he explained, "I was now an A and B student and my relationship with the teachers was better because they were my peers." He leaned forward and added, "I could related to them. I went into service and I came out with aspirations to pursue more schooling and I wanted to be there. I didn't have other things on my mind like when I was in high school and society was putting me through things."

As I listened to CM, I asked him about his family life. His family included his parents and his four younger siblings. "They were poor," he said, "but had enough food and their basic needs were taken care of." He recalled the love they had for each other and how it helped him as a person. He smiled softly and reflected, "looking out for my sisters and looking up to my parents helped me as a person, we had a wholesome relationship by not having much, in that, one helped the other. I guess having each other made us feel pretty decent." His father was a self-employed carpenter. His mother worked as a health care worker and also did domestic work to support her family. She was the person he felt he could discuss anything with and stated, "She always had the time to sit down if I asked her. I might admit that I was a mama's boy. There was nothing we couldn't discuss and she never made me feel humiliated or stupid by voicing what was wrong." His feelings about his father were more puzzling and he never fully discussed their relationship. However, I suspected his reluctance was important to the story. Both his parents were disciplinarians. He remembered their punishments; verbal and whippings, whatever fit. Then he explained, "I think they took it a step further, even though every black family was involved in that. Their interpretation of raising kids was to have them be independent period." He recalled the siblings' extraordinary self sufficiency and collaboration. "We were taught to run the household; iron, cook, and clean. That's why I didn't excel too much in sports because I was at home. In fact, I was more an expert at ironing than with a baseball bat. But I was ashamed to admit it then. We kids had to work, to free them (his parents) up from their responsibility of caring for us." He leaned back in his chair and paused, then informed me, "In terms of responsibility at home, if things didn't go well with mom and pop being satisfied, forget it. And that wasn't the way other people were raising their kids. If we wanted to get out of the house to play or something, we had to take care of the house first, then get the homework done if there was time." After the army when he was 21, and returned home his parents who had grown apart, separated. "I think we were pretty much molded by those years," he reflected, "because even my younger sister had gone her own way by that time."

When I asked CM to picture himself as an adolescent, I was informed that he was very mischievous. "I got into a lot of things but I was fortunate not to have to suffer from it. You would think with so much discipline in my house that I would be a child of God. I was just the opposite." It seemed that the more he got disciplined, the more he rebelled. "I would get some kind of whipping and I would be thinking then and there how I was going to get my revenge," he said. In school he wasn't a good student. "My attention span wasn't what it should be." When he was 14, he worked for a white grocer as a stock boy. He couldn't hide the bitterness in his voice when I asked him about their relationship and he said, "He was a white man, so I could only have one relationship with him. I had to call him mister and his kids, mister and misses, and so forth, and let them tell me what to do all day. It was that kind of relationship because if it were any other, you wouldn't be there." Then he added, "You didn't want what would come to you if you didn't have a good job. They (his parents) called it staying out of trouble. I gave all my earnings to my mom and she bought groceries, school supplies and stuff. But once she let me go to the real barbershop and daddy didn't have to put that bowl on my head. That was my reward for earning money."

His early memories of the places he used as an adolescent took him back to various activities, the YMCA retreat center, the church vocational school, school track and band, and the Boy Scouts. He may have joined his various activities as a way of escaping his own feelings of inadequacy when I learned that the adult leader's of each of these activities were friends of his parents whom he identified with and felt supported by. But, it was the Scouts that he joined when he was 13, and participated in until he was 17, which he described as having the most impact on him. As I listened, he explained, "I really felt good about going to the scout meetings. They offered quite a bit with outings and learning. I found when I was learning something, I really felt good about that. I liked to learn but the structure in school of learning on the blackboard and bringing in a report wasn't my way of learning. I needed things illustrated to me in a certain environment and I sort of clicked with scouts." As I listened to him, I learned he loved the overall feeling scouting gave him when he was involved in a project. He explained, "I think internally I felt somewhere along the lines something in scouting would rub off on me even if I didn't want to pursue scouting. I had visions of maybe one day when I came back to it, I could be a scoutmaster." Scouting became for him the center of his adolescent social development. He said, "You learned a lot of things like having aspirations and moralities which probably weren't taught at home. You were lectured on how to treat your fellow scouts and how to help each other, such as when you were in the wilderness and there were dangers out there and you would need to accomplish a lot. But, if we didn't have any compassion for one another, we would all suffer. So, when we came together as a group, we felt a certain togetherness."

Interviewer's observation. As we ended the interview, I thought CM's recollections of group helping found in the scouts echoed the experiences that he revealed about helping one another among his family members. He felt scouts gave him structure and he enjoyed the involvements of overall projects with his peers. But it was the way learning was illustrated to him in a nurturing environment that he found attractive. I suspect the military had the same effect with its structure, hands on instruction that he needed, and insulated environment. But it seemed even more enhancing for a youth growing up in the pre civil rights south where real limitations of support existed. He concluded by saying to me, "I think I picked up a lot on how together feels, even now, just from those years."

4.1.6 Case Profile #6

Introductory remarks. JH represents the men who grew up during the fifties in northern small towns. Like many of the men he had two settings, one Black, the other White. He is interesting as he shows why the men needed black settings to counter inequalities in their lives. His discussion of both his black and white settings are explicit in how they molded his achievement oriented skills. He exemplifies men who had to deal with the complexities of their youthful identity while being influenced by both Black and White settings.

JH. JH, 56, is a high level administrator for the city's Human Services Agency. A tall, rangy, dark skinned man, his features display the high cheek bones and distinctive nose attributed to his Native American heritage and the wide mouth and generous lips from his African American origins. His eyes appear calm and penetrating at regular intervals. He is a gregarious man who smiles often. Articulate, he speaks with unusual intensity. When we sat down in his living room one afternoon, he revisited what he called, "the images of his childhood."

JH grew up in a small Midwestern town during the late 50's. The town, a sleepy college town, was also home to several small factories, which produced small goods and machinery. With a population of 20,000, about 200 blacks lived there. They had emigrated from the south to the town during the late 30's seeking employment and worked in the factory and service industries. Most of them stayed to raise their families. He spoke disparagingly when he indicated that the town's black families lived in a few white neighborhoods or segregated near the railroad tracks. He lived in the latter. The town's blacks, as I heard from many of the men interviewed, had their own social and support network within the town. Their children, however, attended the white schools and had black as well as white friends. JH bitterly commented on when he and his white friends parted ways as they became adolescents. He said, "the neighborhood that I grew up in was an integrated neighborhood. A couple of my best friends were white guys. Once we started to mature as teenagers, there was a noticeable difference in the relationship. We kind of knew we couldn't be buddies any more. They began to have their own social events and we weren't invited. It was then we learned that as black kids, there were certain things we could do and certain things we couldn't."

I came to understand the inner conflicts stirring within him as he talked more about the town and said, "I was pretty much satisfied with the community, even though there were not a lot of minorities." He remembered the town as congenial as long as blacks knew what they could or couldn't do. When it came to anything, JH always challenged himself to be the best, or at least, do the best he could do. He excelled in academics and sports and competed hard against his peers. As he expected, the harder he tried, the more he got judged for his merit. In high school, JH was placed in the "college bound" program and remembered being the only black male in his classes, which left him with white kids all the time. When he joined the high school basketball team, there were blacks in athletics but not in his classes. JH recalled his exposure to the whites saying, "I learned a lot about getting along. Sometimes, maybe, I didn't like those boys, and I wasn't even the best of friends with them until I wound up on the same team or the same sport and they were forced to get to know me, and I (was forced) to know a lot more people than I would have otherwise." JH continued, "So, I'd walk to school with them, see them after school practice, and then walk home together, and establish a pretty good relationship." He remembered that his teachers and coaches respected him because of his athletic and academic skills. But I sensed his tortured existence when he added, "Even though there were certain things that maybe they did to us and we kind of overlooked because we were black, still there was the respect that we had for them and that they had for us. At the same time, knowing that there were boundaries that we couldn't cross." But against all odds, he responded well to what was required of him.

When I asked him about his black community, he embraced the notion that it was a "protective environment" of specific places such as his church, and Sunday school which were within walking distance from his house, and his core of "black friends" and their families that have remained friends throughout the years. In retrospect, he saw both his communities, black and white as responsible for making him strong in his efforts to achieve. The white community made him try to prove himself worthy. The blacks played an even bigger role and helped him to focus and direct himself and taught him how to win and that the skills of survival were essential. He explained, "I would kind of look at other people, see what they accomplished and try to put myself in that position. . . and try to determine how they managed to get to that point and do it myself." Most of the time he felt he was competing against himself which helped to fuel his adult successes and perspective.

When JH talked about his family, his great love for his mother and grandmother (both deceased) was evident as his voice was thick with emotion when he described them. I learned his close-knit family was comprised of his father, mother, two sisters, and two brothers of which he was the oldest child. He was reared in a modest house near numerous cousins, uncles and aunts who visited often for family dinners and get togethers. The young cousins often played together. His parents, although "poor", as he described them, went on with ambition, discipline, and educational pursuits to pull the family out of poverty as the years passed. His father was an assembly line worker who made a decent salary for blacks back then. JH had modeled himself after his dad who was a disciplined, reflective, caring, family man who carefully weighted his actions. He respected his father's work ethic and for teaching him that his life was what it was, unless he changed it. He remembered that his dad was always willing to listen to any of his problems and advise him. JH was conscious that the things he did were to please both his parents.

His mother grew up in the town and had attended the town college for a year before she dropped out and married his father. Her cousins who preceded her were all college graduates who moved away from the town. He described his mother as "a great lady, very smart, warm, loving, and giving with a great personality which charmed everybody." He went to her when it came to academics and making decisions about himself. His mother, the oldest child of her family, came from an extended family background of hard work and education, and pressed the same values upon her children. Later, after all the children grew up, he said she returned to college to complete her degree and up until her death, she worked as the special assistant to the governor on human rights issues and became a town leader.

JH's grandmother was the family matriarch and the oldest sister of five siblings who had journeyed from Mississippi to settle in the town. His sibling's bonds were deep and loving. Yet, they were all ambitious and very competitive and went on to acquire the trappings of middle class. JH watched his great aunts and uncles compete against one another vying to get the newer car, bigger home, or better job. Their success value system was passed on to each new generation. JH's mother's brother was a product of the family and worked hard too. His uncle owned a successful barbershop, held many properties, and was well respected in the town. JH admired him, tried to replicate him, and sought him out for advice on making decisions about his life. With his siblings he was close and being the oldest, like KP, he tried to set a good example for them as he explained, "the things that I did, I did with them in mind, hoping I could lay the groundwork so that as they got older, they could maybe even do better than I was trying to do."

He remembered the unique role his maternal grandmother played in his life. She taught him about right and wrong in the world he lived in. She was a fair skinned, god-fearing, strong willed, savvy woman whom, he smilingly recalled, always dressed as a demure, genteel southern lady. His grandparents were the family's foundation and as the oldest grandchild, JH was his grandmother's "pupil" and she taught him the family's strategies of survival. Bemused, he remembered visits with her as his life lessons as she used to say to him, "Don't you have any sense at all? People can have all the book sense in the world, but they just don't know how to apply common sense to get a lot further ahead than people with book sense. Baby, learn to trust your own instincts with your books. . . they will be right." As he looked back, JH summed up his family as responsible for teaching him a set of success values and a belief in himself explaining, "there was nothing that maybe I couldn't do if I put my mind to it."

Along with that, he recalled that he gained a certain level of self-confidence that came from knowing he was loved and that he was capable. From that, he was prepared to let the world know.

JH, like KP and TC, described his adolescent self as a rebellious challenger. When he was in high school, he always challenged his friends, both black and white, by trying to be one of the best in whatever he did. He seemed poised on a tightrope, working hard to deal with the contrasts he experienced; the unspoken standards required for acceptance by his white teacher, coaches and friends, and the winning standards of survival by his family. He was bright, athletic, strong willed and directed. But he also admitted that he was a fairly private person who, he said, ". . . never really discussed everything with adults. . ." but instead, observed those around him and tried to figure out how to do likewise. He explained, "I was naive about a lot of different things and thought that the world was, I guess, like a Baskin Robbins store full of 31 flavors of ice cream, and I could have any one of those flavors that I wanted. As I got older, a lot of things dawned on me, such as I couldn't do everything I wanted to. For various reasons there were obstacles placed in front of me. Some I could overcome, some I couldn't, but I had to keep trying."

When I asked JH about the adolescent places he used in his town, he named many involvements. Of course, there was the school basketball team, which he deliberately joined for access to a college scholarship. It taught him a lot about setting goals, being a team player, and learning about people different than he. Frustrated, he remarked, "black guys that made it through high school and went on to college or service were all members of some athletic team. The ones that didn't, dropped out. . . the one's that never went out for anything or never did anything, just didn't seem to make it for one reason or another.

I concluded, as he continued, that it was another place that had a lasting, impact on him. It was the church, he informed me, where he attended Sunday school and was a member of the junior choir and missionary ministry. Specifically, it was the missionary ministry, which JH described as a community center where black adolescents could be together. Convinced of its impact he clarified, "It was a gathering place in the black community where there was little else to occupy kids' free time. We could play different types of games there and they always had some type of educational movie to show us about different things, and we could dance or socialize and give our parents a chance for us to be out of the house. We thought it was ours because it was in our neighborhood, you know, and kids from all over town would come there. I think I still went down there after I got older." He further explained, "We black kids grew up where we didn't have any place else to go and do anything. If you weren't involved at the church center, there just wasn't anything left for you that was good to keep you from getting into trouble." Whatever the impulse, very early, JH and his peers used the center, in effect, as a way of escaping the ravages of race, with all its limitations and humiliations. They needed to be vindicated to find their niche and the center was capable of reaffirming that they were "somebody". JH ended the interview by saying, "It was those ties between the center and our church which reinforced what our parents, family, and neighbors had told us, "As blacks, if we tried to do the right things, good things would come to us. Sometimes we had to wait for our rewards. We couldn't not study, not join activities, or not get things done and expect gratification. It was something that we all needed to be encouraged about to know that in the long run we could be black and get our reward." He smiled and added, "the Godly part of me taught me that first you needed to learn to be happy with yourself, then you wouldn't have to worry about the rewards coming."

Interviewer's observation. JH speaks poignantly about his experiences growing up in his community. From his community, his friends, and their families he gained his patience and coping skills. From his family he learned the moral and social values of hard work, perseverance, and a solid religious foundation. His personality reflected a determined, logical youth who saw the class and race distinctions of his life. And, from his settings, both black and white, he learned skills too. From his experiences on the white team he learned how to be a part of a whole and get along with diverse people. From his black setting, he learned that in face of the humiliations of race "good things would come in the long run through hard work."

4.1.7 Case Profile #7

Introductory remarks. KP represents the men from small town segregated southern neighborhoods during the pre-civil rights era. His transformation from being a "boy who believed in justice to a civil rights agigator" is reflective of the impact of important adolescent settings on many men. His group setting was a dance combo that he played in with his brothers on the weekends to supplement the family income. He credited that experience as his first real opportunity to bond, share, and work as a team with his brothers. He illustrates the monumental need black youths had to relate to each other in their efforts to develop their identities and survival skills.

KP. KP is a 54 year-old; slightly built dark skinned man. He has intelligent eyes, a quixotic smile, and he is surprisingly soft-spoken. A lawyer, he is an advisor to Jesse Jackson and Nelson Mandella, and a tenured law professor at one of New York's most prestigious universities. Early one morning, he and I sat in a restaurant across the street from the university as he revealed to me his life story with an unusual reflection and intensity.

KP grew up in a tight knit black community within a segregated small southern town during the late 50's, at the onset of the Civil Rights Movement. His town is located in tobacco land and is the county seat. During slavery, his part of the state held more slaves than the rest of the state. The town's blacks were the direct descendents of slaves and the town was the home of the KKK and where the John Birch society was founded. He remembered that the town's blacks stayed to themselves socially within their own community of schools, churches and gathering places. In this black community, he emphasized, he and his peers' families were linked to a core of teachers, neighbors, churches, and friends within a needed social support network. His memories of school and his teachers proved important. He recognized his teachers as community leaders who left the town for college and returned to teach, inspire, and make their students excited about learning, and more importantly, the knowledge that there were other ways of life. He remembered his world opening up through the readings he was assigned and clarified, "I could journey to far away places and pursue extravagant dreams I never thought possible. . .." In retrospect, he realized that the teachers were preparing each child to stand up as "ladies and gentlemen," he said "against racism." He added that it was because of the teachers that each of the town's black youths went to college and became participants in the movement for equal justice. He told me that out of adversity his community was able to offer he and his friends a core of people to give him direction, leadership, and validation.

Within the town were KP's family; his mother, father, and his three brothers of which he was the oldest. Although his parents had married at an early age, they maintained a strong family unit. The family lived in a private house and ran a dry cleaning business that eventually failed. He described the family as "poor, but always having enough food, love, and material goods and close ties to extended family members." The family was musical and everybody, including his uncles, aunts, and cousins were talented vocally or instrumentally. "Every afternoon," he commented ". . . our front parlor was a very active place as my parents, brothers, relatives, and me held musical concerts." As he recalled his father, KP offered an observation and a distinction as he described him as a soft spoken, quiet man who in his early years struggled with alcoholism and irresponsibility. Through the efforts and support of his wife and family, his son remembered, his father stopped drinking and "became a quiet, disciplined man." "His strength," his son commented, "was about law and business." When KP was in mid adolescence, his father was sent to prison for what his son called a crime he did not commit. It was that event, and through the urging of his mother, which led him to his decision to become a lawyer and stand up for the rights of black people. After that, KP remembered the outdated law books that his mother would bring him to read from the white lawyers she worked for. He described his mother as a calm, proud but directed woman who was the family leader who made sure that her four sons would be prepared for the dangerous world away from family and community. KP said his mother was open to her sons and they could tell her anything. Because she was a "very, very personable and quick woman, everybody in town respected her." This allowed her to be a quiet agitator for the rights of black people while she molded her son to be a strong voice. Love of church, education, hard work, and self were the values that she instilled in her sons. And when they were young, she took them every day to the "colored" library to expand their minds through learning. She frequently reminded them to be proud of who they were and strive for whatever they wanted to be. KP wanted me to know that he and his brothers never dared to defy their parent's expectations or requirements or act irresponsibly in relation to one another. He attributed to his family, immediate and extended, the gift of a needed value system of structure, discipline and determination that he carried throughout his life.

KP remembers himself as an amiable adolescent who, although always bigger than his peers, behaved as his family and teachers taught him. He explained, "I didn't fight, steal, cheat, or bother my friends." As a student, he worked hard to please his light skinned teachers whom he thought knew everything. As a dark skinned boy, he found his own way to be accepted and prove himself to his light-skinned teachers. He explained, "mother would say just wait until after the first exam." So, he excelled academically and socially and ran for and won the presidencies of his class and school band, and led many of his school clubs.

His cheeriness changed when he was 17 and he had to stand up to the bitter challenge of racism in his town. KP described his involvement in a dispute over the town's annual Christmas parade. Traditionally, the "colored band" had always marched at the end of the parade. KP felt the tradition was unjust. Supported by the black community and some whites, he organized a threated boycott of the parade. Later, he and his teachers eventually met with members of the town Chamber of Commerce where he presented his position. To his surprise, they agreed to desegregate the parade and the town was eventually desegregated too. He modestly informed me, "... from that incident, I went from being a boy who had believed in justice to being a civil rights agitator. ..." From his victory with the town he was written about in newspapers across the country and sought out by Dr. Martin Luther King, Jesse Jackson, and Eleanor Roosevelt who later became his friends.

When I asked KP about the adolescent places within his community that he used, he named several, his football team, church, high school band and a dance combo. He named an unusual refuge setting as being the most impacting on him, his dance combo, in which he and his brothers played six nights a week at a local nightclub to help support the family after their father was sent to prison. His mother supported him and his brothers' involvement with the combo with certain stipulations. They included that they did their homework during the intermissions, kept up their academic standards, never smoked, drank, or cursed, and kept a Bible close at hand. KP and his brothers enjoyed their popularity and being known as fabulous musicians. Even more, he liked the brothers' musical association and the alliance that they formed together. From their experience, two of his brothers would go on to become internationally known musicians in adult life. "When my brothers and I played together" (in their place), he said, "it wasn't the entertainment or the performance that counted for us. It was being together regularly that closely to become 'best friends,' to talk to, share, and learn from ..." KP went on to define the brothers' combo as a focused opportunity for the brothers to bond, share, and communicate. He used a metaphor to explain. "I had my brothers and we were the music with each brother a note, not separate but a part of the whole that would be incomplete without the other." He felt that they learned as a group to appreciate each other through the structure and organization that their performances required.

Interviewer's observation. At the end of our interview, key themes were revealed as KP informed me that he recognized that the blending of support from the people in his family, community and his refuge setting had made it possible for him to be where he is today. He explained that the whole of those experiences strengthened him and never allowed the rejections he felt and received in life to ever make him feel inadequate or dissuade him from his goals.

4.1.8   Case Profile #8

Interviewer's remarks. RJ represents the older men. Raised in his southern segregated small town nearly a quarter of a century before KP, by his widowed mother, his setting was the black church which became the center of his early life and work. His patterns show us the variety of coping styles the men used to survive racism. In his case, he employed the survival styles of conformity and respectability.

RJ. RJ is a tall, stately, immaculately dressed and very dignified man. We met early one morning in the kitchen of his large brownstone in Harlem just after his wife had served him a southern breakfast on silver pointed dishes. He speaks clearly and articulately with a flair for the dramatic which is so common to black ministers. He is 72 years old but appears 10 years younger, and is retired from the ministry, a former divinity professor, former founder of the Bronx chapter of the NAACP, former state administrator for a redevelopment organization, and a man who once had dinner with President Harry Truman. He looks forward to our meeting as he informs me that he is in the process of completing his memoirs for publication.

He was born and raised in a small segregated town in Mississippi during the late 20's. The youngest brother of four children, he lived with his older brother and his wife and children in Louisiana from age 11 to 13. After his mother became ill when he was 13, most of his adolescence was spent in Mississippi when he returned home to care for her. RJ and his mother lived in a private house in the black part of town. The town, the county seat, was a small village of about 1,000 people that included the wider range of surrounding farms and woods where most of the black people lived. His early memories are that "Every one of the town's people knew everybody else." He explained, "So, there was more intermingling between the races than the usual southern town and less harshness." He could still picture the town's whites as freer with blacks than in other parts of the South. "As a kid," he said, "I worked for a white man in the town's drug store and he used to kick me behind the prescription counter and say you get from here. You've got a good mind and you go out and use it." He explained, "People didn't say they mixed, but so many of them did. And that was a part of the era that no one heard about. In our town, there were some mean whites and some very fine whites. We were never a part of the lynching or any of those experiences." He hesitated, then told a story of a black woman who got into an altercation with a white woman in town and the woman's husband tried to whip her. "The black woman's employer, who was also white, drew his gun and threatened to shoot the man if he struck her. That kind of relationship was found between most blacks and whites in town" RJ commented. He described the town as, "this group of black people and this group of whites who came out of Reconstruction together." He then quoted his father saying, "What a great start was made, but it was frayed in the process."

The town had three white high schools and no high school for blacks. He lamented that education kept from blacks was one of the deficiencies of the state. He smiled softly and said, "So, for black adults and their children, the church became their center of life and work. You started off with that as a small child, there was no such thing as a black child not going to Sunday school; that was a part of your growing up." He called it "the place for everything and you went there for church, Sunday school, and school. The church's black school was a one room school held in the church." For him, it was the place he learned about his black background. "That was drilled into us," he said, "just as my father had taught me." "In school we'd always have speaking situations and marches where they sang, "We're marching through Georgia, hooray, hooray. Sing the jubilee the flag that made us free. We will sing the course from Atlanta to the sea while we're marching through Georgia." He smiled and explained that from his school song, he learned, for the first time, about General Sherman and the Civil War. Later on, when he talked more, he remembered on old man named, Uncle Wash Thomas, a former runaway slave, who would sit all the children around him and tell the story of General Grant and slavery, the struggle, and the war. He added, "And he (Uncle Wash Thomas) had his old union uniform, and he drew a pension from the Federal government. You see white people who fought didn't draw pensions because they were Confederates and that was impressive to we kids. As

I listened, I suspected that comparison led the youths to believe that black people could, after all, play important roles in life. "There were two things I knew, he commented, "the Bible and the background of the Reconstruction. It was drilled into us." But he also said, "blacks taught but didn't know that much so they had to fend for themselves. Most of the young blacks had to leave town for education. When they returned, which was seldom, except for the church's first Sunday in August, they came from everywhere and the community had protracted meetings with them with the best food and they'd hear stories about their schools and jobs and what they'd learned." He revisited those comforting images and responded, "I loved the world that my community offered."

When I asked him about his community friends, he said he had two sets of friends, his cousin and his white friend, the nephew of the town's richest man. He and his white friend would go to each other's house (uncommon then), and ride ponies that were given to each by the boy's uncle. He and his cousins would go to the black church revivals and events together or to see his uncles or friends or their families on their farms where they would explore. He said, "We'd drink clabber (cow's) milk and eat cream." "We would roam together," he said, "and my mother always wanted us to dress correctly." "We used to wear white duck pants and go around to revivals, the theater, and the junior church."
His face beamed as he proudly described his family.

His father died when he was 10 years old but he remembered him well as a great churchman and advisor for many of the town's blacks. "People used to come to our home and talk about things. Black and white from all over the state and sometimes they would stay the night." "One night," he shook his head, "two guests, a white man and his son stayed until the early hours of the morning and caught the train after conferring with my father all night."

His father had been married before and had older children from that marriage. His mother helped raise them and they, in turn, helped her raise RJ after the father died. His mother was described as brown skinned, and his aunt was darker. But his cousins were very light-skinned. He found out that the family was the offspring of the union of two white brothers and their black women who couldn't get married. They all went on to live together on these plantations and the heirs got the land. His mother, he remembered, was one of the most discerning people he ever knew. She taught her children the basics of life and was very much into planning for her son's existence. Her three sisters, like many of the people in his extended family, also had a lot to do with him. One especially would take him fishing and tell him stories of slavery. Another aunt always took him places. He shook his head saying both his mother and aunts, although not well educated, believed in education above all other things, and his mother insisted he finish high school. He informed me, "When my mother recovered, some of the people in the community agreed that their children would live with her for a week and so forth, so that I could return to my brother's house and finish school." He went back to Louisiana to do so and lived with his brother. Most of the town's blacks were related and his parent's cousin's lived nearby. They, like the rest of the family, were more well off than most blacks and had farms and property of their own. He responded, "Now cousin Hiram was father's first cousin, and he had a whole lot of land. And then there was my mother's cousin, Sophie; she came up to our house with a surrey. You know with the fringe on top; she always tended people. Then another brother went to court and got his hands on the Shell plantation."

When I asked him what he was like as a youth, he described himself as a thin, inquisitive, bright, and a very determined student. As I listened to him, it was clear that the town's blacks admired him for going to school. He remembered, "One year, cousin Hiram said to me, "Here are five acres of land. You are in school (high school) and you can plant them. I planted two acres of corn and three acres of cotton. A man came by from the Department of Agriculture and they bought it and gave me the money." His eyes sparkled when he said appreciatively, "I used it for my schooling."

He ended the interview with these final thoughts as I asked him to reflect on his lifepath. It seemed he believed his life successes were tied to his community. He leaned forward in his chair and said, almost reflectively, "All of this seems to have been tied with destiny and destiny is not something that's accidental to me. It is guided and you can't do it without other people." He commented further and summed it up in this way, "So, everybody, from my mother and father, to Mrs. Hanks in the church, to the school and Uncle Wash Thomas, to my whole background, the town, neighbors and family, all were willing to give themselves over to trust what I could do." RJ looked reflective, then added, "The main thing that happened is the black church and school got us started. It made sure we had no end. It didn't decide what we were going to do but it got us thinking and from that if you get people thinking, they will do the rest. They can make it and so forth." "Surrounded by family and friends, we thought we had three things going for us," he said, "one was the church, the other was having our minds centered on the teachings of Jesus who is straight forward, and progressive in all He did which wins anywhere. The third was education."

Interviewer's observation. RJ's story was interesting because he reflects men who grew up in the era of segregation when the inequalities of racism and discrimination were devastating. Yet, like most of the men, he was able to supersede those negative influences through the buffer of his family, community, self, and settings. Although RJ's community was racist, he was able to take the positive elements from within, such as Uncle Wash Thomas' stories of slavery and his relatives and parents to remind him that he came from a proud community of survivors. RJ's character, being "brighter" than most children, allowed him to experience the world of his white friend, and a desire for getting a college education. And the church which RJ called "the place for everything" drilled into those Black children that they could play important roles in life in spite of the circumstances they had to endure.

In the profiles my purpose, in particular, was to examine the everyday lives and nurturing behavioral settings that a core group of high achieving black men used as adolescents on their lifepath to achievement. Central was to show how exposure to enriching environmental settings empowered them as black youths, and installed self esteem and success values to yield high achievement outcomes. I wanted to find out what part their settings played. What did it offer them? Did they get adult role models, instruction, goal directed behavior, values, positive motivation, or all of these? Accordingly, did their settings trigger or did they only reinforce the participants early goal directed behavior?

As I listened to RJ and all the men, I heard many central themes. First, the men needed people who comforted and supported them. Second, their paths were of hope and purposeful design. And, each in his own unique way was able to buffer his rejections and nourish his thirst to achieve. Also, race was a principal variable affecting the way in which they viewed their situations. Thus, the way that each man coped was defined and enhanced by their racial identity and affected the style in which the conditions that they experienced were confronted.

Their communities, through a social network of their families, and the places they relied on as refuges, offered them diversified opportunities. These "refuges from racism" measured them by standards that kept them from feeling compliant or self-satisfied. Finally, what we find are environments that stressed hope, aspirations and possibilities as they redirected racism into winnable situations. For many of the men, settings acted as their "finishing schools" teaching them the skills they needed to confront to transcend the conditions they endured.

In the end, we learned that the hard struggles of their survival were contrasted against and mitigated by the vitality, energy and drive that they all shared. What is key is that in relational terms, their varied personalities, families, community backgrounds, and safe places were coordinated to help them to negotiate their adolescence and bridge the difference between their black community origins and their upper class destinations.

What follows will be a more detailed account of the positive directed influences the men experienced through their neighborhoods. Also, I discuss their characters and academic levels, as well as the impact of the negative influences of racism, drugs, and crime. Chapters VI and VII probe the types of settings that the men used and what their settings were able to offer them. In Chapter VIII can be found my conclusion and a summary of my findings. Then there are the discussions of the limits of my research and its implications for future reference.

5 DISCUSSION OF RESULTS

5.1 THE ROLE OF THE MEN'S ADOLESCENT NEIGHBORHOODS IN THE SOCIALIZATION PROCESS

5.1.1 Description of Neighborhood Types

The eight profiles attest that from an early age, black male youths are socialized to form their survival strategies, coping mechanisms and forms of resistance to racial discrimination and class bias by home and the larger black community (Allen, 1981; Staples, 1983; Wilson, 1987) that they confront. In some ways their issues are usually quite different from other youths that are not black or of more middle or upper class backgrounds. In this context from the men's comments, it is obvious that many viewed their neighborhoods as built on the common needs, talents and contributions great and small, of its residents. As such, within them its members reflect a need to share and aspire through a network of relationships which offer and affirm their complexity and worth.(McAdoo, 1989). In this chapter, I examine how the men described to me their perceptions of their adolescent communities. How these varied neighborhoods differed or were similar in impact was the crucial concern.

Eight men came from racially mixed communities where blacks lived in their own enclaves. Of those men, five lived in large urban northern cities. These men were found to be younger and ranged in age from 29-44 years old. The other three men came from southern urban communities. They were older at 45-51 years old (see Table 8).

Most of the men, 17 men, grew up in segregated cities. The breakdown was relatively even with eight men from northern urban cities and nine men from southern communities. Of those nine men, two came from southern urban cities and five from southern small towns. The rest, two men came from Guyana but had moved to the States later in their adolescence. The southern men's ages had a wide variance and ranged from 49-77 years old. The northern men were younger and ranged in age from 29-61 (see Table 9).

The men described neighborhoods that generally were made up of communities exclusively black with the central social contrasts of fine homes and dilapidated housing -- educated people and uneducated people -- hard working people and those who did not work.

It was easy to get a sense of the men's relationships to their neighborhoods. When asked about its physical features they spoke of neighborhoods that established the boundaries of their social universe. Also, they confided about their frustrations and anger as well as their favorable memories living within their communities (see Table 10 in Appendix 1).

They seemed to share a certain sameness of life and their common place in the economic order where concentrations of relatively poor or low-income people lived. However, I learned that the boundaries of their neighborhoods, while created to hold them inside, became defense perimeters as well. As such, each secured a border within, which made its inhabitants feel a sense of belonging.

In this context, I examined the relevant features of the men's neighborhoods and tried to identify what supports they felt were or were not available in them. In the end, I hoped to gauge the impact that these specific environments had on the men's ecological patterns.

Parents Residential Patterns By Neighborhood Type

The majority of the men had two parent households located in clearly defined settlement patterns.

5.1.2 Location of Father/Mother Households

Of the 18 households where both fathers and mothers resided, six were found in northern racially mixed, urban (3), and small (3) communities and two in a southern urban racially mixed neighborhood. The rest, ten households, were found in segregated communities. Of those, four were in northern segregated, four in southern segregated communities, and two in urban southern segregated communities. Men whose parents resided in racially mixed communities in the north were shown to be younger men who ranged in age from 38-44 years old. Men from the South were older at 49-72 years old (see Table 8).

5.1.3 Location of Single Parent Households

Of the eight households where single mothers, widowed fathers or single mothers and other relatives resided, two were found in urban, northern, racially mixed communities. Another resided in an urban, southern, racially mixed community. The rest included two men from a segregated, urban, northern community, one man from a small segregated town and, and two men originally from Guyana. The two men who lived in the north in racially mixed communities were younger and raged in age from 29-34 years old. Older men came from urban, southern, racially mixed communities (one man, 46 years old) and in northern urban, segregated communities (two men at 51 and 61 years old). The oldest man, 77 years old, was raised by his widowed mother in a small segregated community (see Table 9).

5.1.4 Location of Other Parent Households

Two of the men were raised by others. One man was raised by his grandparents. The other man by loving foster parents. Both men, came from urban segregated communities and were respectively, 29 and 50 years old (see

Table 9). In the next section, I look at the men's perceptions of how their neighborhoods influenced them.

5.1.5 Perceptions of Neighborhood Influences

Colemen's (1988) concept of social capital was found evident in my research which suggested the ability of neighborhoods to shape adolescent life courses. The men spoke of communities that created the social relationships they needed to implement their goals (Furstenberg, 1993). It appeared in turn that these neighborhoods played potentially important roles as reservoirs for the adolescents' social capital.

Closer examination provided detailed accounts of what life was like. They all agreed that they were seeking places to play, opportunities to socialize with friends and to "escape" from the emotional battering of the larger society that branded them "invisible" and offended or undermined their sense of self.

They spoke of travelling to and from their homes without adults, often in small groups of best friends. In urban areas they described violence, drugs, and crime as the negative images of the neighborhood. In the South and other places, segregation and inequality were remembered contemptuously. But, I learned that each man became deeply familiar with the complicated elements of their neighborhoods; the policeman, drug dealer, Klansmen, local grocer, poor people, rich people, middle class people, and individuals who made up the communities social fabric.

They reported that they needed adults to listen to them and foster their need to share and learn survival strategies and experiences. Without such relationships, each man, was unprepared to critically assess his social reality through trusting his own voice. In these circumstances, I saw them as neither taking their community for granted nor recoiling from it. In most cases, they became alive to threatening situations and developed ways to behave. From interactions in their neighborhoods, they became something more than passive reactants to situations. Instead, they became proactive, and to some degree authors to their own actions.

Northern urban segregated. The majority of the men (8 men) grew up in northern urban segregated neighborhoods. The most noteworthy descriptions that emerged were (a) everybody knew everybody, (b) it was a unique place, (c) it was robust and full (d) it was closed off from the rest of the world, and (e) it had a lot of community.

Steps were taken to unravel the complexity of the neighborhood's impact on them. When I spoke to TC, a 28 year-old Legislative Aide, who grew up in the early 80's with his elderly grandparents in Harlem public housing, he illustrated the complexity of his community.

> ... we lived in public housing and my grandfather was about 75, and president of his senior center for years. Sundays were about sitting with him and his friends listening to them talk about history, politics, and food. And they would quiz me on history and Napoleon... I was always with him. I still remember my best friend's telephone numbers from then. ... now we are all around 29 years old and work, but most of us still live in the complex but

> now we're involved in trying to improve the community and make a difference for the people who live there. ... the neighborhood kept us together... a lot has to do with economics and real estate.

TC explained to me about his reference on the neighborhood's "economics and real estate." He based the term on the low median income represented by a majority of the community's residents. His plan was to work politically to assure that rehabilitation plans for a community, which holds some of the city's most historic and well designed housing stock,be returned to its original attractiveness. He based his thinking on the dramatic influx over the past decade of higher income black and white residents who had moved back into the community, and to the increase of positive print and media coverage about the community. When I asked him about the negative images that he remembered about his complex during his adolescence, after a brief silence he continued about the harsher realities.

> ... there were gangs in the neighborhood... real wild boys with violence and fistfights but I was never approached to be in a gang. But this was the age before crack, so if you got in a fight no one was going to pull out a gun and blow your brains out. Besides, I was very busy with my involvments in boy scouts, sports, and school...

Northern urban racially mixed. The second largest group (6 men) lived in New York City in racially mixed, ethnically diverse neighborhoods. In these neighborhoods the men reported the "invisible" but known boundaries of each culture. But, they all agreed that they had everything there even with the diversity of racial and ethnic lines. One man, BB, 46, an engineer with the Metropolitan Transit Authority (MTA) who grew up on the upper West Side of Manhattan near Central Park during the late 60's illustrates the point.

> ... we had a little bit of everything. You had Columbia University's students, then the little corner between 110th and 108th was black folks and they were ghetto folks, and downtown below 96th Street you had rich white folks which made me realize I wasn't middle class, I was poor. Another section, 103rd Street was Spanish, and they had a bit faster lifestyle that I didn't want to get into... drugs, and stuff like that.

Clearly, BB struggled to live in a world of contrasts. I marveled at BB's willpower and self control because although he lived in a multi-racial and multi-class neighborhood, he seemed to have found his niche by playing football for his neighborhood team. I was struck by the fact that he conceived himself as living up to the standards which were not his alone, but those of many in his community no matter what lifestyle, which validated youths being star ballplayers. BB went on to say:

> ... I didn't want to get into the fast world and I didn't want to get into heroine... I remember one day my friend and I were walking through Central Park and we found an American flag and we started walking with it. All of a sudden, we were surrounded by about five guys cursing at us, and they took our flag and were going to beat us up. Then one guy stepped forward and said 'no, no, no, they're all right, they go to school and play football'. Some

years later, the kid that saved me became a drug addict and overdosed... but that day he was my hero... and I suppose in a way I was his...

Southern small town segregated. The other large group (5 men) lived in tight knit rural small segregated communities. They were remembered as isolated, focused places where everybody knew everybody else. When I asked RJ, a 72 year-old minister, former divinity school professor, and organizer of the Harlem Urban Development Corporation about his adolescent community in rural Mississippi during the 30's, he articulated for me the subtle threads of racism that many of the men endured. He said:

> My town was the county seat of Franklin county with a population of about 1,000 people including the wider range of farms around... it was all segregated but there was some intermingling. I remember Aunt Jenny who raised the Hollinger children and Uncle Wash Thomas who had been a slave. He used to gather all the black children around and tell us about it... and there was the church, the place for everything. It was a part of your growing up and direction... I once remember Mormons came through our town and I wanted to meet them. I was told I couldn't meet them because I was black and this was disheartening because even though we had been taught about racism, now I found out it was even in the church.

RJ's poignancy illustrated the harsh realities of life for black people in his town and historical period. When I asked him how he insulated himself from such tensions, he spoke of being told by the whites in town that he had a good mind and should go out and make something of himself. He also credited his family as being pivotal because they were "well respected in a way," with his father being a "great church man," and his mother a "lady." Then he proudly remarked that his "best friend" was the son of the town's richest white man. I came to understand that RJ, like many blacks of that time is best understood as having seen himself protected from his pain. To him, the mantle of respectability as a mode of life seemed to embody his notion of moral worth. Constantly made aware of his plight, he was encouraged to be different than most of his race. Required not to complain or be bothered about whatever reactions he might have about the racism of his environment, he complied. It was from these early painful experiences that in his later adult life up North, he founded and headed his state's first chapter of the NAACP.

Southern urban racially mixed. The next category of two men lived in Southern racially mixed cities. For them, their neighborhoods had "a place for everything and compatible friends." JC, a 51 year-old psychologist, and one of the men profiled in Chapter 4, thought about the boy he had been and about all the people who lived there and helped him. He remembered his early 60's neighborhoods in this way:

> I grew up in Lynchburg and it was like a protective enclave of black folks. We had no fear there of anything because the men had guns and the women knew how to do things. They built their own houses with their own hands, and most of them were teachers. My parents were teachers too, so,

they were all friends. From them, I learned early on what the game was all about...

JC showed that within the town important distinctions were being made between blacks and whites. Later on, JC's parents took teaching jobs in more urban Baltimore and his nurturing environment changed.

> When we moved to Baltimore, I was just stupefied... the white kids would not play with us, so my neighborhood life revolved around playing basketball with the black kids from sun up to sundown, so we were always a group. In school I was taller... I was smarter and I could play basketball better than any of the white players. The white teachers couldn't stand it... so it was a good transition for me.

In thinking about being black and competent, JC, who later went on to graduate from Yale, like so many of the men shared experiences of rejection and how to absorb racial blows early on. Clearly, I noted the highly embattled sense they had to overcome in interacting with the outside world. In spite of that, JC, like most of the men shared an even more intense willingness to work even harder to prove themselves. And, as JC said to me, "I had to constantly remind myself that my special mission was to move the race forward."

Northern small town racially mixed. Three men lived in northern, small town, racially mixed communities. Within these racially mixed communities they lived in segregated black enclaves or in a series of houses within a block of white families. These enclaves had their own social network within the larger community. One man, JH, 56, profiled earlier as one of eight men, is an example of these men. Another man, DD, a minister of his church's youth church and a Yale graduate grew up in a small New Jersey town during the early 60's when the style of segregated living was still in practice. He described his town in this way:

> I grew up in Jersey City, New Jersey. We had a very clean community with very friendly neighbors. At first our neighborhood was integrated but it gradually changed and became predominately black with an influx of black middle class people moving in. My parents were both ministers at our local church. We had what was called a block association, and for many years my father was the president. Those were the good years because on a monthly basis, the community would come and gather in our basement... so I saw strong leadership in action there, and I saw their presence in the block was really making a difference. Then we would look forward to the annual block party and get kids from all over and have games, tournaments, and what not. This was before the drug age, you know, good times. We were children and grew up without a desire for negativity like so many young people today. How different it was then to now.

When I asked about the negatives of the community he said:

> Well I can't recall anything that was really negative. I mean it was so good. I went with and married the girl next door. Now you don't even know whom the girl next door is. Right now, I can't say a lot about any negatives.

Like the other men of this category, DD found life in his black community caring, supportive, and encouraging. This view seems consistent no matter what region or time period the men came from, with the exception of CM who found his community repressive. CM's view follows.

Southern urban segregated. Two men lived in Southern, urban, segregated communities. One man, CM, 49, who was also profiled earlier, reported his experiences in his pre-Civil Rights hometown left him with little hope to excel as an adolescent. It was after he left his community that he felt willing to achieve. In another view, RG, 65, a highly successful entrepreneur came from a middle class family of ministers and grew up during the post war years in his Missouri community. He too, left home after his graduation from high school to excel in the North as an adult, but fondly remembered his adolescent black community as inspiring. He said:

> I grew up in Missouri in the city's black community of about 500 people. It was close-knit because everybody knew everybody else. Parents would work five days a week and on Sunday, everyone went to church. There were no movies, parks to play in, or any other entertainment; that's what we did on Sunday in church. We might spend time in the library and a man named Mr. Mack, who ran the grocery store knew every child's name. In high school they wanted every child to be able to meet academic standards and they took time with us. And if you went into trade, you had to have knowledge of that. The teachers were really a part of your life from the day you walked into school to the day you graduated because those teachers were also our Sunday school teachers. So, they made us prepared and became a part of our lives. In church you went through all the Sunday school classes together with your peers. In all, you always got a sense of security and direction in our community.

Rural/other (Islands, the USA). Two men grew up on the island of Guyana but had relatives in the states. After hearing about the promise of success here, their parents sent them here in their late adolescence (17 years old) where they lived in low income black communities in Brooklyn and Queens. The parallels of their lives on the island and in New York showed similarities to the other men. Each spoke of working parents and community members who wanted them to do well in school and have good professions. These men too endured the obstacles of poverty and class. One example is KK, a PhD and educator, who is 49 years old, and grew up in Guyana during his early adolescence. He described his poor, rural, black community in this way.

> I look back on my community as a second family. It was very inclusive with relatives and friends close at hand. Everybody surrounded you so it was very good. We knew that we could not do anything within that area because visibility was good in terms of supervision. Everybody supervised you and we were protected. I loved that, everybody looking out for everybody else. It helped me because the focus was on. . . you better be good. Now I can look back and see the respect, the encouragement, and the discipline. I really did enjoy it. I had many friends there but we knew that opportunity lay in North America. . . education wise, financially, and professionally.

When KK was 17 years old, he came to the States to live with relatives.

Through these simplifications of the men's experiences in their hometown, most reported encounters with and similar reactions to racism. Yet, their experiences also revealed positive supports found within their communities, to counteract negative racial images that they endured and clearly felt in their anger and frustrations.

Although the men's individual neighborhoods were disadvantaged, each was able to offer a variety of social supports that provided help, caring, diversity, role models, and places that treated them in accordance with the images they had of their own worth and value. In their minds their communities, because of the persistence of racism, became yardsticks with which they measured their worth. Indeed, most times they found inspiration and affirmation in their relationships within their black communities. In turn, their communities contributed to their perceptions of them as insulative, protective and influential in setting the stage for their own self-empowerment. In many cases, the men said their neighborhoods socialized them through interactions with peers and adults and provided the positive support influences they needed through a network of available supports. The fact that they did so no matter what type of neighborhood, region, or historical period is significant.

5.2 THE ROLE OF FAMILY IN THE MEN'S ADOLESCENT SOCIALIZATION PROCESS

5.2.1 Description of Family Background

The men's adolescence could not be studied without considering the interaction that occurred between the multi-faceted environmental systems that they operated in. They included the nuclear family environment, peer groups, the neighborhood, and other outside influences. In this section I focused on and examined the youth's most proximal environments: the family. I did so because each had a hand in determining what the adolescents did, whom they did it with, and how they felt about the interactions.

I was aware that the positive attributes seen by youths in black communities are collective phenomenon in which some values are instilled by the family -- some by the community and peer culture and some by schools and other institutions of the community such as churches, and various youth centered organizations. At an early stage, my goal became to investigate the ways in which one of the ecological systems -- the family goaded the youths towards using settings.

Although theories of communities generally ignore family management, clearly, the men's families were pivotal by teaching and modeling behavior that played a crucial role in the development and maintenance of each of their early characters. Thus, a main concern was to measure each man's motivation from home which led them to supportive settings and away from negative influences.

Through my conversations, I learned about their families, their parent's employment history, and their relationships with their parents during their adolescent stage. Based on the literature's profiles of black family models, I had expected to find family backgrounds that ranged from quite supportive to not very supportive. My findings disconfirmed the stereotypes as the men's families had a number of positive factors to foster their son's access to desirable settings and, in turn, effect their long range outcomes.

My examination of the families found that generally most had well defined parent and child roles (parents fulfilling concern for their children's needs, rather than their own). Secondly, parents seemed to combine a competence and an awareness of their children as they exercised informal social controls that encouraged their sons and gave them the opportunity for greater self-direction and potential, as fully as possible for self-realization. More importantly the family had an effect on their education for racial socialization and teaching them how to survive. The men did not come from stereotypical mother-only households. Indeed, the great majority (24 of 28) came from traditional two parent households. These parents were remembered as stably employed with the exception of one man's parent, and importers of a strong sense of security and traditional values which placed strong emphasis on hard work, perseverance, and ambition. The men, although "not rich" by economic standards, reported being "poor" but quickly assured me that they "always had what they needed." I learned that "what they needed" was love, caring and support in a collaborative effort by family and community adults and peers.

Four men's parents ran their own businesses and two were college graduates. But generally, the men agreed that blocked employment opportunities and education because of discrimination led to most of their parents having "blue collar jobs." Parental employment patterns showed fathers were laborers, farmers, truckers, barbers, and pastors. Ten of the men's mothers were homemakers with fathers reportedly working two jobs. However, the rest, 18 mothers, held jobs as maids, clerks, and teachers. Tables 11-14 in Appendix 1 summarize the more important employment and parental type characteristics examined.

Most of the men were very aware of their parents' lives and used them as models for their adult roles. They said their parents were concerned about their future and encouraged and supported them, which enabled them to go out into life and be "somebody."

What follows are retrospective recollections of the relationships the men had with their parents. And, too, the type of environment they felt their parents provided for them.

5.2.2   Father's Role

Men without fathers. Sociologists (Wallerstein, 1991; Moynihan, 1990; McLanahan, 1985) stress the importance of male-models for the development of high attainment and rational expectations for young men. In this context, I found fewer than 25% of the men (4) reported not being raised by their fathers. Of those four, three of them were raised by their mothers with another male relative who acted as a father figure (step fathers, older adult brothers, uncles, or grandfathers) in the household. The fourth man reported being raised by "loving" foster parents from 14 years old to adulthood. Four other men were raised by mothers only. Three of these mothers were divorced, and one woman had never married.

Men with fathers. The strengths of fathers who lived in the home proved significant. Seventeen men described dads who were workaholics and stable role models for their sons. Yet, while their sons tried to emulate them, the theme of appreciation for the father's influence became at times coupled with expressions of frustration and some anger. One man, CC, in his mid-sixties and the father of four college-educated children, and a retired juvenile justice administrator, recalled his father as a very stable person with a total commitment to his family and his farm. Because he was a hard worker, his son reported, he expected a great deal from his children. CC, like many of the other men, expressed appreciation, admiration and some frustration as he poignantly explained:

When I graduated from high school my father in a polite way suggested that I leave the farm. He said that if I stayed on the farm, I wouldn't work. To that end, I was fortunate to get a baseball scholarship because I hated working on the farm. At the point I went on to college and he (his father) gave me what represented all he could afford which was five dollars... all he had. I never forgot that.

Similarly JW, 53, who also grew up in the South and is the owner in partnership with his wife, his childhood sweetheart, of a network of New York City beauty shops which consider the customer's comfort first, remembered his businessman father in a town that had few black businessmen. He observed that he modeled his own business approaches after his father who believed a black man could be whatever he wanted to be if he just worked hard enough. He said:

Father had a barbershop in the white community (the only black man who did) and he taught me values such as how to treat customers and how to respect your wife and family. He showed me the value of hard work and from him I learned how to respect and help others. I would work in father's shop until evening and help shine shoes, brush people off, and he paid me which I saved in part for the movies and dates. From father, I learned kindness, professionalism, and respect, to tip my hat when ladies go by. I have tried to be like father in my work and family life.

Three men reported fathers who were hard working authoritarians and not close to their sons.

One man, JM, 54, a Wall Street Securities Vice President, and the father of four grown children contrasted JW's memories of his father with his bitter memories. JM described his father as "a taskmaster" who belittled and demeaned him, only to support him when he went to church or got good grades. JM explained:

My father, my father's father, my great grandfather were all ministers. I was basically involved in all aspects of the church because it was approved and I could get away from home, from my father. He would allow us to go to church and I was there seven days a week, and a member of everything. Father worked two jobs to care for us. But he was strict and a lot of people in the community were scared of him and he tended to scorn me if I did something he thought was wrong.

When I asked him more about his father, he revealed an inflexible man whose ways damaged his son's self-esteem and added:

My father and I didn't really have a good relationship because he was very authoritarian and dictated what you did. When he said you cleaned, you cleaned... yes sir, no, yes... he used to use the razor strap to keep us in line... we (he, his sister and his brother) were scared of him.

Fathers who worked irregularly. In contrast, 3 men described their dads as "dawdlers" who lost their jobs regularly. But even those fathers were remembered as being involved and loving fathers.

For example, GM in his late fifties, the widowed father of two sons, and a lawyer and former college vice president illustrates this type as he shared with me about the warmth and patience his father showed him.

Father never learned to read or write so he used to wash cars at the car lot. As the years passed, his capacity to work got less and less. But he was my pal and he looked after me until mother came home from work. We shared the same dresser drawer for our clothes and he did the cooking and I got to hang out in the afternoons with him and his friends as they gambled sometimes, and I would loan them $5.00. I had then a lending operation going on from my savings.

GM was convinced that his close relationship with his father led to his own loving and involved parenting style with his sons. GM's experience parallels another man's, FB. FB is 65 and the father of nine children, and he reported to me that:

Father was an oil truck driver but he had an offensive nickname, Crapshooter. All the children kidded us about that name. But father provided for us and loved us all.

Because of this father's offensive nickname, FB recognized that in later years he came to admire his father's willingness to be a good provider for his family. Like GM, FB in trying to make sense of his past, credited his father's model to his own behavior as a hard worker and stable provider for his family.

Fathers out of the home. Five men reported fathers out of the home through divorce, abandonment, separation, or death. Three of these men were raised by single mothers. The rest by grandparents and foster parents.

5.3   MOTHER'S ROLE

After learning the father's impact, I wanted to understand what role the mothers played in the men's life choices. So, I examined their recollections of their mothers. I was concerned because most literature on black mothers generalized their impact as either stereotyped "stressed out" single mothers or the "driving forces" behind their son's eventual successful outcome. Hill (1996) concurs and placed great significance on black mother's roles in his analysis of the lifetime achievement of 100 successful black men. He found that it was their mother's love typically reflected in each one of them. My findings showed that while the role of the men's mothers was significant in their son's lives, generally, their role as "driving forces," was disconfirmed. Instead, most of them showed interest in and stabilized their son's behaviors more so in partnership with their spouses than not.

When one looks in detail, 18 of the 28 men reported mothers who were supportive but low key in motivating their behavior. Only 3 were reported as too busy to be involved (see Table 14, Appendix 1).

Mothers of less influence. RC, a church administrator for one of the largest black churches in the country and married to the first female chaplain for the City of New York shared his experience and illustrates this type of mother:

Mother was very witty and had a lot of mother wit about her. She had a slight stroke that disabled her, so there was not much she could do. I was like her personal errand guy. I ran errands for her because she was disabled and stayed close to home. My stepfather was there for me and he worked. He was a strong man and he taught me so much about life, and my father taught me about love.

Mothers as driving forces. Seven men described their mothers as the single most influential person behind their achievement. With respectful but conflicted resignation they told how their mother's determination and constant pushing fueled their first desires to achieve.

One man, JHS, 29 and Chief of Staff for one of the state's most powerful senators, made a simple but powerful statement as he discussed his relationship with his mother, who as a single parent, pushed her only child. He told me:

> Mother was a teacher and a college grad and she made me go to the library regularly with her where she would read the NY Times to me. Here I was only a kid... she wanted me to have middle class aspirations and graduate from college and get a professional degree just like she did. And I was supposed to become a lawyer.

In another example, GMD, 60, and a lawyer and university dean who grew up in Harlem, had a similar experience with his married mother. He had stated that his father worked erratically but described his mother in this way:

> Mother worked as a draper in the garment district downtown. She understood hard work and she had goals for me. You've got to be better educated than the white boys she said. She would compare me with the sons and daughters of the men who ran the businesses in her work. Then she said these are the things you have to do to set your goals. She set the limits and watched me like a hawk. She had these middle class aspirations for me and I had to juggle a lot.

A third man, KM, an architect, spoke of how his mother's impact on his life and how it supported his desire to avoid the negative influences of his West Baltimore neighborhood. His mother was described as making him believe that any change at all in him had to do with his having something to hope for. He credited his mother in this way:

> Mother always believed in me. She prayed for me. She told me I could be anything I wanted to be.

Single mothers. Five men had no fathers. Their mothers were the primary caregivers. An examination of these mothers led me to conclude that the majority of them did indeed fit the literature's model of "stressed out." Their sons confirmed that life circumstances left them too busy with the extra burdens of lowered incomes, increased economic insecurity, and family care to devote to a nurturing relationship with their children. Most of the men said these mothers had less control over their children and did fewer activities with them, leaving them at most times to their own devices. These were also the men that seemed drawn to peer-controlled settings without interference from other adults.

PD, 35, a commodities broker on Wall Street who grew up in the south Bronx, makes precisely that point as he tried to understand his mother in this way:

> Mother and dad separated when I was 10. Mother became the provider and she worked hard and made a lot of sacrifices for us all. My goal was to look out for my younger brother and sister as mother was always tired when

she came home from her job as a dietician. After Dad left, I felt as though I was the man of the house, and I had to set good examples for my siblings. I didn't go out and do a lot of things the kids in the neighborhood were doing. I had a good relationship with my sister and brother, and mom needed support. I wanted to reciprocate what she did for us and so the chores were not designated, it was something we all knew we had to do and we did it to help her because she was always so tired.

Possessed of more pointed resentment, BA, 45, an engineer and a dedicated family man, and father of two spoke of his experience with his divorced mother in this manner:

Mother and father split and I grew up as the little man of the house. We were on public assistance and mother and my three sisters were party girls. I fought with them always about their lifestyle and I didn't want to be like them. I had freedom of the streets but I found my role model in the guy who coached my neighborhood baseball team. . . he carried himself so well and respectable.

In BA's case, escape from his home's values, rather than support by them directed him to his community setting. And escape from being like his mother and environment became his driving force.

For PD, he sets in motion a description of the survival strategies that the other men used to toughen themselves up against resentment of estranged fathers and overwhelmed mothers and their relegation to parenting siblings. Later, in my conversation with the men, I learned their refuges seemed to be their group of friends where they could become just boys again.

The interviews of all five men revealed how much they needed another parent. But I wondered if their mothers were exhausted from working, emotionally distant or tried to teach their sons how to be tough to survive.

For all the men studied, again and again, they named their family's support or the circumstances of their families as a key factor in shaping their goal direction. Largely, most told me it was their parents, no matter what class they were that upheld respectability and middle class aspirations, that in some real sense gave them solid values and encouragement towards the material attributes of success and support for whatever they wanted to be. I am convinced that in most of the cases, the men's stable family values also encouraged high standards of achievement in them. Thus, family life became a determinant to assist them in developing more positive social orientations and searched to form partnerships with added goal reinforcing opportunities, whether in school, church, formal, or informal neighborhood settings.

In the next section I examine the roles their own personalities played in their outcomes.

5.4 OTHER FACTORS RELATED TO PLACE USE

5.4.1 Resiliency and Adolescent Personalities

In face of the social realities of the millions of black male adolescents who live in black communities and allow themselves to be doomed to poverty and failure because of some force over which they believe they have no control, I focused on what forces enabled them to beat the odds.

As researchers we know that coping skills may not develop in a vacuum. And while one person may develop such skills, another may not. I suspect that developing skills may be particularly associated with having different experiences coupled with the personality to seek effective social supports. My interest was the relationship between personality and one's willingness to seek support.

The men showed that their teen characters were shaped by their experiences with people and situations. And character cannot be taught directly but must be experienced. Clearly, each man's adolescence was a series of small events, periodic conflicts, racism, and discrimination. The responses they had were not without consequence but determined who they would become. But it seemed their early ambitions were to be survivors.

I began my inquiries by exploring what traits reinforced the men's beliefs that they had something special in them. I concluded that it was when they decided to take responsibility for their lives and become agents of their own change instead of being acted upon.

Most of the men described themselves as hard workers, persistent and competitive as adolescents. A few surprisingly, characterized themselves as socially introverted, which changed after using the settings they recalled as important. All agreed that their settings helped them to reflect on who they were and what they wanted to become. And the literature shows that black men who do accumulate success have similar traits (Hill, 1996).

Thus, it seemed likely to me that the men's adolescent characters may have been at the pivotal point of their transformations. Indeed, all of them challenged the negative impact of racism and made choices to channel their energies into involvement with positive personalities like themselves, and accept the social capital that was offered to them through their settings.

Given this view, it seemed to me that any deep examination of the men's adolescent development required insights on their individual personalities. If so, personality may be considered a plausible variable in the transformation process. Thus, they were asked to describe themselves as adolescents. What follows are the traits they identified.

5.4.2 Self Perceptions of Adolescent Personality Types

The varied facets of the men's adolescent personalities were in their perceptions of themselves. I wanted to determine if any patterns of similarity or differences existed between regional locations or historical periods, and if individual personality predisposition helped the men to direct their selection of places. To obtain the data, I asked the men to describe themselves as adolescents. They did their narratives with a general degree of affection, humor, and some pathos in their recollections.

Five predominant personality types emerged. They were competitive and enterprising for 15 men, and shy and quiet for 6 men. A third group of seven men categorized themselves as rebellious and questioning (4 men), and socially cheery (2 men). another man described himself as a dreamer/adventurer (See Table 15, Appendix 1).

It is evident that each man's way of coping with their environments was correlated to their personalities. I found in each man's coping, an involved making sense of his lived environment rather than being victimized by it, whatever the difficulties. And, too, it reflected that with their resilience they needed structured environments.

Predominant personalities versus place of residence. Fifteen men described themselves as **competitive, enterprising** personalities. Ten of those men grew up in northern communities and I found it significant that seven of them were raised in New York City where competitiveness is seen as part of the norm in daily life. The other eight men came from both southern and northern communities. Interestingly, the age range of men from New York City spanned widely, from 28-61 years old as did men from other northern communities with ages ranging from 38-56 years old. But the oldest men, ranging in age from 51-77 years old came from southern communities. I suspected that their competitiveness was shaped and encouraged by their black communities, families and settings in a network of supports to endure racism. Competitive/enterprising men grew up to varied professions ranging from politicians, lawyers, army colonels, and Wall Street securities directors to ministers, bankers, engineers, and businessmen.

Six men reported being **shy and quiet** personalities. Five came from New York City and ranged in age from 34-53. Another man came from a Southern community and was 65 years old. When I explored further, I learned that 4 of the 5 men from New York City grew up in public housing. Three of them were raised by a single mother. The fourth man, respectively by his mother and stepfather, and the last man by a domineering father and loving mother. Shy and quiet men grew up to be church administrators, architects, and businessmen.

Four men reported being **rebellious and questioning**. One of the men was younger at 29 years old, and raised by his single parent, maternal aunt and her son in a racially mixed neighborhood in New York City. It was his mother's constant involvement with the direction of his life, he reported, that led to many of his rebellions. Another man was 65 years old and grew up in the south on his parents' rural farm. he reported he hated everything about his life of farming. When he was 18 years old, his father financed his way to college. A third man, CM, was 49 years old and hated life for blacks in his racially torn southern community. The fourth man grew up with a single mother who struggled to raise him and his younger siblings in his drug and crime ridden community. These four men grew up to be the chief of staff for a senator, a juvenile justice administrator, a real estate developer, and a Wall Street commodities broker.

Two men reported being **socially cheery**. Both were middle aged at 51 and 52 years old and raised in the South. both came from two parent families with supportive relatives nearby. Both of their parents managed black businesses and were well respected in their black communities by both blacks and whites. I suspected their cheeriness and even temperament which is evident even today, saw them through many of life's obstacles of racism and discrimination in their pre-Civil Rights communities. One man became a widely respected lawyer and law professor at an Ivy League school. The other became a wealthy northern businessman.

Only one man called himself a dreamer/adventurer. he grew up in a tenement in Harlem and was 52 years old. He mused about not being as 'smart" as his brothers and friends, and the main child care provider for his younger siblings while his divorced mother worked to support the family. He grew up to be an amateur playwright and writer and later the public relations liaison for a major New York City public utilities agency.

How the men reacted to their environments given their personalities intrigued me. The diversity of their personalities is illustrated below.

Competitive and enterprising. Fifteen men described themselves as competitive. TB, a gregarious man who grew up in a large and loving home in Harlem with his divorced father, aunt, a multitude of cousins, and his grandmother shortly after the Depression is one example. He laughingly responded this way:

> I was always into stuff and I was very competitive. I would make sure that I could always do better than you. I just knew I was somebody and I was very precocious because I lived in this household full of adults and I was the youngest person in the household. It was very interesting to me because I could sit down and listen to their conversations every night. Their love lives, the economy, and the job market and it was a learning experience for me because they were all wonderful people who had made miserable choices in their personal lives. it was a really big family situation.

During that period, A black professional couple moved into TB's home which would change his life he said, and added:

> This was my first close-up exposure to a professional couple that was black. My family had hard working people but when we rented to the couple, they couldn't find jobs. I followed this couple and joined their chess, orchestra, and opera clubs and I was appreciated for myself. I wanted to emulate them because they dressed and spoke so beautifully. When I came home because I had street English, they would constantly correct me. I think it was a combination of looking at how hard my family worked, my own sense of awareness and what I considered a dreary life for my cousins and not wanting to duplicate that.

From observing the couple, he said, "I wanted to change my character; I became a lover of the classics, and I began to read expansively."

Shy and quiet. Six men acknowledged that they were shy and quiet and generally spent time with one or more close friends close to home. PD is one example, he is a 35 year-old Wall Street commodities broker who grew up in the Bronx in the shadow of Yankee Stadium. As the oldest of three siblings, he cared for his sister and brother until his divorced mother came home from work. He gave a glimpse of his personality in this way:

> I was very shy and quiet and really didn't smile a lot because I was missing a tooth in front. Mother was willing to have it fixed, but I didn't want to. My father had been an engineer and mother a dietitian and we were middle class then. After they divorced, mother worked very hard to support us. So, I stayed with my three friends from the complex near the house and

helped her with chores although they were not designated. I felt as though I was the man of the family and I wanted to set a good example for my brothers and sister. I didn't go out and do a lot of things that a lot of the other kids did. I was more a homebody except for playing basketball.

Then he added:

Guys from the neighborhood would play basketball seven blocks from my home near Yankee Stadium. It was a convenient location, and we would talk about school or the neighborhood or just watch people coming from Yankee Stadium. I was a star player on the team and I got to travel to other gyms to play other teams. My coach (someone from the community) was very patient. He wanted everyone to play basketball and go to school and get an education. I began to express myself more and be a bit more open and gain confidence in my abilities.

PD spoke candidly. He seemed like someone who felt estranged from his environment but found solace and encouragement in his settings of friends from the neighborhood basketball team.

Rebellious and questioning. Four men fell into this category. One man, JHS, a young man in his late twenties and Chief of Staff for a powerful legislator grew up under the watchful eye of his mother and aunt. He leaned back in his office chair, reflected for a moment, and then described his cynicism and aloofness towards adults. He said:

I didn't have respect for adults having all the answers. Mother had always treated me as an adult, so adults had to prove to me that they knew better than me. I was always asking questions and always skeptical and challenging.

When I probed further, I suspected the way he was raised was responsible for his mistrustful attitude that had begun to keep adults at arm's length. Later, his group experience in ROTC seemed to positively channel his rebelliousness.

Socially cheery. Four men recognized and appreciated their social skills with other children and adults. KP, 54, personable and an attorney, illustrated this personality type well. He said:

I had some personality. Everybody liked me and I tried to be nice to everyone because I felt I was going to be President one day, and they were all potential voters. As a child, I was always bigger and stronger than the other boys but I never had any problems with them. I got along and I was well known as a musician with my brothers, and cheery. I didn't lie, steal, cheat, or bother anybody.

KP illustrates the men of this category. Like he, they took into account what they felt they needed to get ahead and adjusted their personalities accordingly. KP for example, as a cheery youth continued in this way through his association with his brothers dance combo where he reinforced his knowledge of how to satisfy the needs of the group as opposed to self. In his later teen years, he became involved as a young civil rights agitator who fought for the rights of blacks in his town.

Dreamer/Adventurer. Only one man, RT, a personable man, described himself as a dreamer personality type. He grew up in Harlem where he, too, cared for his younger siblings until his mother came home from work. He explained:

> I was the slowest of my three brothers. The oldest was the smart one, the youngest, the cute one. So, I felt all the problems that come along with being the middle child. I carried the burden with me and I was introverted, imaginative and a late bloomer. I was curious and would make up stories while going through a difficult, questioning, angry time for me (his father left home).
>
> One of my high points was across the street from my building in a vacant lot. I was a latch key kid and my little brother and friends entertained ourselves until mothers came home from work. We used that vacant lot as our ball field and we played softball and stickball there. Also, we had our little fantasies. . . we pretended that we were jet planes and that the lot was an aircraft carrier. There was a lot of creativity there, a lot of imagination, color, livelihood, and pain shared.

RT seemed sensitive and regretful about having less to offer than his siblings or friends. He alleviated his own sense of low esteem by dreaming in his vacant lot setting. RT went on to write plays in his early adult life, and today he is the community relations officer for Con Edison's special projects.

Sometimes as I listened to the men, I felt that their adolescent characters sought places to complete and refine their potential. Clearly, there was a correlation between their taking responsibility for being led to their places and how the places were used by them. The men's character traits varied considerably and the variance is understandable. At times, it seemed that they were different and worked through to success in very different ways. But a major factor in each of their successes was the reinforcement of their individual motivation, drives, and desires to survive.

What struck me, however, was how they used their individual styles to work through obstacles to their success. From that process, they were able to create place cultures based on their own individual needs, and in turn, these places helped to shape them.

5.5   Academic Levels: School Environment

Historically, for blacks, education has always been a power and of great value. In this regard, the social and economic progress that blacks have made in this country has been in direct proportion to the educational opportunities available to them (Polite, 1992; Hill, 1988; Mincy, 1994). Thus, I chose to examine the relationship between the men's personalities and their reported academic standings. Generally, high school in this country is the central organizing experience in the lives of most adolescents. Through school and the use of both academic and social activities, adolescents are given the opportunity to learn information, and master the skills important in their later life.

The men all agreed that they were led to believe by family and others that if they worked hard and were determined, with a little bit of luck, they would succeed. But black youths face formidable challenges to their educational development as their aspirations, pride, and achievements throughout school systems are seriously stifled. The men revealed accounts of competition and persistence in white school settings that sometimes required them to endure much rejection on their paths to acceptance. Those who attended black schools had fewer resources and teaching materials, but most still excelled. They also spoke of their desperation from just being adolescents. Still, in most cases, they were able to have a positive attitude towards education and generally achieved in school despite obstacles. This seemed to create a powerful motivation for them and revealed resilience and clear understanding of the value of their education.

Analysis of the men's academic standings contradicted some of the stereotypes of the literature (Shepard and Smith, 1989; Gardner and Lipsky, 1993) which suggests that black males from low income communities have more need for special instruction education than other cultures. The findings revealed that of the 28 men, 25 (89%) had higher than normal academic levels. Nineteen of those men (68%), were classified as "gifted," 6 (21%) above average and 1 man was an average student. The rest, 2 men (7%) said they were poor students but improved in early adulthood during their college years.

Sixteen of the 19 gifted students reported they attended schools outside of their communities. Another 9 men reported placements in the "college bound" programs of their black schools. Of the two men who reported being poor students, one attended a black school in the segregated South before the Civil Rights Movement and the other, attended catholic school in Harlem. Those men who reported attending school outside their communities found them not to be nurturing places but places where their "color" was never forgotten. Being black, they also had to cope with racially rooted barriers. Faced with hampering school experiences distinguished at times by ineffective teaching strategies and educators with predetermined negative views about their learning potential, all the men emphasized they worked hard to prove them wrong.

The basic difficulties that they encountered best illustrated by FK and GMD who both attended schools outside of their communities. FK is a 52 year old retired army colonel. The only child of his laborer parents who lived in Harlem, he was a bright boy in school but his teachers at his white school never reached out to him. He said:

> My high school was predominately white and considered the next best thing to a special school for the gifted. So there were not a lot of black and Hispanic kids or teachers there. I never developed any kind of relationship there with the teachers or students. As a result, I don't have a recollection of any teacher in school. In my black school, I had been somebody, I found out unfortunately I wasn't there, and it was disheartening. So, at 3 o'clock I got out of that building, put on my cadet uniform after school, and went to Minisink (his neighborhood setting).

Another man, GMD, 60, a lawyer and former dean of student affairs at a major urban university said much of the same:

In my school, I was an academic star and ended in classes with nothing but whites. I was like the only black in those classes and it was quite a transition from Harlem. I did okay in the classes; as a matter of fact I did fine. but it was the early nurturing you know that helped me to have a sense of myself there because there was no nurturing. I had a determination to do all the things the white folks did. And it wasn't looked on well because I was the antithesis of whites there.

I came to understand that the degree to which the men struggled to stay connected to school and education in spite of the alienation was fairly common. Yet they showed resilience as they explained that school and the opportunities for learning and competition were their first references to the "outside world" and better futures. Similarly for them, it became their training grounds for learning skills and civility in unfavorable environments. Too, education became the key to their strong sense of self-esteem and for their personal and collective power. It was not an easy enterprise but the men's patterns of integrating place and personality development prevailed.

Not all the men showed early signs of promise. Two men described themselves as poor students and agreed that schoolwork never came easy for them. The first man, CM, was a 48 year-old real estate developer who grew up in a segregated community in New Orleans. He ruefully admitted that he didn't try to compete in his black high school because he was doubtful about his academic abilities and any future opportunities for their use:

I wasn't a good student in high school. My attention span wasn't like it should be and I was rebellious. I felt the need to be an individual and I didn't wanna go to school. . . the teachers were not that supportive either. Later, in college, I became an A student.

When I probed further with CM to understand the frustrations that led to his poor grades, he revealed that it was rare to find any professional people in his black southern, urban community. Most of his friend's fathers, he said, were unemployed a lot. He attributed his own lack of self-motivations to that environment, even though his parents were employed and encouraged hard work for their children. He regretted that in later years he might have been more if someone had been around to tell him he had potential and explained, "I didn't have anyone to support me to go to school, so I thought if I could get away from that environment with the expectations I had, I could make things work for me."

The feeling of powerlessness that CM conveyed was common for most blacks in his pre Civil-Rights community and seemed to bring forth conditions to stifle his ambitions, lower his educational efforts and set up barriers to his doing well in school. The end result was his dismay and rebelliousness that like most of the men in the study, still fueled his later efforts to prove himself and work hard.

A second man, RT, 50, a public relations officer with a large public utility company grew up with his divorced mother and two younger brothers in a tight knit New York neighborhood in Harlem. He remembered being a latch key kid who had adult neighbors to look out for him until his mother came home from work. His frustrations lay with his white catholic school environment in Harlem. He told me:

I was not one of the sharp kids in my class and the support systems were not there. The teachers (nuns) tried to help me understand the importance of education but I had attended an all black school before and it just wasn't the same concern and support. Later on I learned the enormous joy that came from reading and the school had a singing group and I could sing which helped me to come out in time.

RT remembered his friends as being better students than he, with parents that encouraged them to study and do well in school. At times, he remembered the parents asking him to go home so their sons could study. It almost seemed that RT tried to alleviate his deep feelings related to his family circumstances and slower educational abilities. The literature is also clear that single motherhood often has educational consequences in poor neighborhoods. That is, as mothers increase the number of hours worked for family financial stability, they decrease the time needed to provide education enhancing goods and services which their children may need (Amato and Keith, 1991).

The research indicates that both CM and RT lacked self-motivation to overcome their school environments. Appreciating the differences of the other men, the presumption is that the majority, maybe because of supports, remembered their school experiences in spite of racism as useful. For them, school experiences on the whole provided them with their first reference to the "outside" world and exposure to other academically motivated youths like themselves in an environment away from the accepted norms of their communities. In doing so, schools became at best for them their training grounds for learning skills and civility in the fact of racial defeat. And education became the key for them to develop a stronger sense of self esteem and, in turn, personal and collective power. No less important was the advantage that all the men created for themselves; the experience of finding favorable environments to help them create stable futures. In the end, I found myself wondering whether the men's outcomes would have been the same if the facets of their individual personalities and the places they used hadn't become integrated to reinforce their way of staying true to who they were in the face of racism.

5.6 The Impact of Racism on the Socialization Process

Although I didn't ask about racism, its theme seemed to permeate the men's narratives. It was evident it was a strong concern. The depth of the nature of their oppression was only revealed after I began analysis of the tapes. All of the men honestly tried to explain how race affected their experiences and lives. Again and again, in every account, I heard the same perceptions of anger and pain. They were deeply troubled by the dehumanization of racism, and they all seemed to ask the same questions: Why were they pigeonholed, treated unfairly, and blocked in their efforts to aspire? The subtle insults and rejections that they endured and had to swallow were emphatically revealed.

In this section, I decided to focus on what I learned. As I listened to them, I remembered Ladner's (1971) observation, which reminds us that socialization for Blacks is always different than that for Whites. Understandably, it is because the race issue is a more powerful variable in a social economic system that has been historically stacked against black youths and prevented them from taking their traditional masculine roles (Staples, 1983; Wilkinson and Taylor, 1977). Without question, I learned from the men that the most decisive factor that they felt influenced their resilience was the widespread expectation of their failure and the oppression that they endured and learned to deal with. And the consequences of racism towards them were manifested in a variety of troubling ways.

One man, CM, 49, a real estate entrepreneur, illustrated the point as he described his experiences growing up in his segregated early sixties New Orleans hometown. For a moment he seemed to become angry remembering the daily inequity and himiliation:

... it was truly segregated. In fact, I grew up in the old school speaking in terms of the black plight. It was yes sir, no sir, and misses, and so forth. . . even their kids were called mister and misses, simply as that. . .

CM's painful overview provided an important commentary and it paralleled the bittersweet memories of another man, JH, 56. JH, like CM who was profiled in Chapter 4, is a human service administrator who grew up in a small northern town during the late fifties. As we sat in his living room, he related it this way:

The neighborhood that I grew up in was an integrated neighborhood. A couple of my best friends were white guys. . . once we started to mature as teenagers, there was a noticeable difference in the relationship. We kind of knew then we couldn't be buddies any more. . . that as black kids there were certain things we could do and certain things we couldn't. . .

Drugs, Crime and Violence

Regardless of the toll of racism on all of the men, those who lived in urban environments presumably experienced even more negative influences. In their conversations they warily identified the devastating tensions that they endured in their communities from drugs, crime, and violence. Trying to contend with these influences was pointedly remembered by the men who grew up in northern urban cities. Many of them spoke of how they developed oasis; bands of caring, comforting places with adults, and peers to counteract negative influences. This process was best described by two men, RC, a 48 year old church administrator who grew up in Harlem during the early sixties, and RT, an administrator with a pubic service agency who grew up in Harlem during the 50's. RC concluded:

I grew up in Harlem. It was a robust, growing, thriving community, full and vibrant. Often you'd see the crowds headed up to the baseball games. Every store along our block was open and doing business and the majority were black owned. You knew blacks owned the cleaners, the barber shops, the fruit market. . . everybody knew everybody else.

He paused briefly, then added:

Then the power (drug dealers) began to take its toll on the community. . . you started to see guys standing in the hallway shooting up drugs and stuff. . . sometimes your mother had to come out and bring you into the building. . . walk over those knuckleheads. . . first drugs, then more violence started breaking out in the community.

I was surprised to hear such solemn, thoughtful words. Yet, in spite of such frustrations RC went to great lengths to inform me that his young spirit was not eroded. In fact, all of the men admitted that in spite of the dangers of drugs and violence and the racist assaults that they endured, they were convinced that they did not feel it deeply.

Their conceptions, however, were clearly not what I found. Instead, their cumulative experiences showed a rage and frustration inside each of them which years later emerged as they angrily spoke of their bitter experiences. Oftentimes it seemed they were left feeling helpless to deal with the attitudes, assumptions, and stereotypes of those found outside their communities that tried to make it difficult for them to achieve. For many of them, no doubt the consequences of being black seemed almost a negative. And such pain dictated a general cynicism of the world outside their communities. To combat the pain, they looked within their communities for places that could act as refuges for them from racism and danger.

One afternoon as we sat overlooking the streets of Harlem, one man, RT, looked out at the street from his office window, paused briefly, and described for me what his neighborhood was like for him:

> Yeah, we all lived within one block of each other. There were ten of us, all good friends and we would covenant to watch out for each other. We weren't a gang... we never got into any violence. We just played ball together, went to dances, and had a really good time together. Our camaraderie and our friendship was enough of a support because we had common interests and you know growing up poor and black, it was kind of difficult to establish any kind of outside relationship. I think we were blessed to have had our group of guys. And the adult figures were there too, because of the children, to look out for us. And the insurance was there because the adults would reprimand their kids, and you would also get the benefit of their teachings.

The men's perceptions indicate how much they believed that their neighborhood settings were conscious of their inherent inequality and the threats of crime. They offered them the nurturing, warmth, and welcome that they needed to counteract the dangers inside, as well as outside, the community that they endured. Weary of people who saw nothing about them but their color or tried to victimize them, the men sought neighborhood places that provided them with a source of collective nurturing, and discouraged any limits placed upon their abilities.

Similar experiences were reported by a third man, CC a 65 year old retired human services administrator. Growing up during the mid forties in his southern community, his talents and self worth were also affirmed by his community. When asked, he explained it in this way:

> I grew up in a very unique little town in the South. It was one of the cleanest places you've ever seen in your life. People in my area (black community) took pride in the city and what it was all about. We had a nice nucleus of friends who were positive role models whose parents were structured people especially in education. Many of them had fought hard to attain a good education and they wanted the same for their children. From the church, there were baseball teams run by the men of the community.

From his and the other men's recollections, I came to understand the subtle and not so subtle manifestations of racism. Also, especially for those in the northern states, I saw it was coupled with the ever-present dangers of drugs and crime.

I came to understand that the standard concept of a protected, carefree and non-responsible childhood was never easy for most black men. Even with love and guidance, in most cases, the men reported their parents were unable to offer them total protection. This may have been in part due in some part to the parent's own vulnerability to discrimination, racism, and crime as expressed by many of the men. In such relationships, it appeared that both generations, parents and children, were inclined to see American ideology in the same light and notably grew cynical and soon frustrated by the inequality that persisted.

The findings suggest that both parents with their children were able to devise their own patterns of self-affirming socialization through the formal and informal gathering places that the men spoke about.

Clearly, at any given moment, the men observed threats to their positive development were constant. And many of the men mentioned to me that in spite of their intellects, they were acutely aware that they were never treated as whites but demoralized by racism and the wall of social resistance they faced. They seemed to have resigned themselves to the notion that Whites were unalterably prejudiced towards them. Hence, they believed that almost any relationship with Whites that was not clearly instrumental was fundamentally a waste of time. More over they observed a racial etiquette based on these assumptions as one man explained, "I knew I was not what white society perceived me to be and I enjoyed proving it."

The action in their lives took place where they felt that they could meet other boys like themselves. What then might be reasonably be considered is that they sought places that like their families and parts of their communities could make them feel safe, challenged, and cared for. In this way, most of the men agreed that their settings gave them collective nurturing to gain inner strength, resolve, and direction for the standards within themselves. In turn, their transformations helped them transcend racism and other negative influences, instead of being sunk by the difficulties they encountered.

Given the relationships of the community men who helped them, the scout leaders, band directors, coaches, or church youth leaders, I found that they involved themselves in, and stabilized the men's lives. These "helpers" were remembered for the positive models they provided as men who believed in hard work and family life, and the men tried to pattern their lives after them. As role models, they were the aggressive agents of the community with the acknowledged role of teaching, supporting, encouraging, and, in effect, socializing the youths to meet their responsibilities regarding work, family, the law, and citizenship. More often than not, they acted as surrogate fathers for those without fathers, or as a third party, to augment the relationship between parent and son.

As a consequence, this network of "others," caring adults and peers in partnership with their families helped to wrap an insulative, protective cocoon around the youths and buffered them from those who did not value their worth.

6 THE ADOLESCENT SETTINGS

6. 1   RECOLLECTIONS OF THE MOST INFLUENTIAL SETTINGS USED

In an effort to understand the effectiveness of the settings the men used, this section examines the unique opportunities settings offered the men. I asked them to tell me about the places they used, what they did there, and what happened to them there. They remembered places that were either formally structured with adult supervision or informally without. Settings described as providing places for play, making friends, adventure, and opportunities for youth decision-making, and leadership were the more utilized. And, I was surprised to learn that places such as neighborhood play lots and playgrounds were the least used.

In most cases, the men recalled their settings offered collective phenomena and it seemed to vary from place to place. Generally settings fit into the domains of the youth's environment and provided ample supportive services to meet their needs. Common were the programs they used to promote endeavors that enabled the men to pursue and enjoy their goal of social and economic mobility. I suspected that the process by which they chose settings often centered on settings that had a diversified network of helping hands. And while most of the men used more than one type of setting, each remembered a favorite one which will be discussed in more detail in the course of the research. The following settings were listed (see Appendix 1).

Table 1. MULTIPLE SETTINGS USED BY THE YOUTHS

Settings Used	# Youths Used It	# Youths Did Not
Non-school based sports group	10	18
Non-school based social setting	9	19
Church/Youth center activities	8	20
School based band, choir, orchestra	8	20
Neighborhood playground, play lot	8	20
Community-based youth center	7	21
School based informal setting	6	22
School based sports team	4	24
School based chess, debate or political club	4	24
School	2	26

When I looked at the favorite and most frequently used setting these data were revealed:

Table 2. FAVORITE SETTINGS USED

Setting Types	# Men Used It
Organized Sports Settings	
(school, church, or community sponsored)	8
Informal Sports Settings	
(neighborhood parks or racetracks)	2
Organized Youth Program Settings	
(ROTC, Naval Cadets, Minisink,	
Orchestra, Boys' Club, Community	
Center, Boy Scouts)	6
Church Youth Programs	6
School based Debate Club	1
Peer Cliques Informal Setting	
(music combo, meetings with friends	
in special places	5
Total	28

In the next section I discuss these findings in more detail.

Overall, the differences of historical period, region, or community type were not found. For example, youths that lived in small segregated communities went to church activities or played ball like northern urban youths. And my presumption that youths probably used more formal settings during the 70's and 80's because more public-sponsored projects were available, proved not to be valid. Notably, of the 7 men who fell within that age cohort, only 4 men used them. One of the programs was school-based ROTC; another, school-based basketball, and the other two programs were community based, boy scouts, and the naval cadets. The rest of the men used informal social settings within the neighborhood such as a playground, or private community spaces.

It is reflected that there were no differences in the men's recollections about eagerly looking forward to being with a group of friends like themselves at their individual settings. When I asked how often and when they used their places, they mentioned having wide ranges of freedom over their daily lives, generally after school when parents and caretakers allowed them to travel independently to their activities. And the concept of freedom as clarified in the literature reports that especially in low-income areas, boys have more access to street life at younger ages. Also, there seemed to be certain roles that settings played. Clearly, the need to be with youths like themselves seemed significant.

When I talked with GM who grew up in Harlem during the early 1950's, he described his setting as a harmonious place. He smiled and said:

> You could go in the evenings to centers, which they had in most of the schools in Harlem... they paid teachers to work in the evenings after school. Then kids could play basketball, shuffleboard, ping-pong or pool... then there was dancing. These activities gave you a chance to meet and talk with other kids. But more importantly for the boys there were things to do there that were important to us like sports.

Other men also spoke of informal places within the neighborhood that they used even when recreational parks were close at hand.

One man, RT, who grew up in Harlem in the early 1960's echoed GM's experiences and informed me:

> ... across the street from my building was a vacant lot. I was a latch key kid and my little brother and friends entertained ourselves until our mothers came home... we used that lot as our ball field. We played stickball, softball, and it was there that we had our little fantasies. I liked to pretend I was an airline pilot and that the lot was an aircraft carrier... there was a lot of creativity found there... a lot of imagination... a lot of color, and a lot of livelihood shared there.

A third man, "TB, who also grew up in Harlem a decade earlier than RT in the early 1940's, saw his settings as a place to get away from his parents and adult cousins whom he described as caring but restrictive at times. His perspective of getting away from adults who had the worries of daily life to give them "space" was widely shared as he recalled:

> ... kids from the block would swim all day in the summer at the community pool or play ball... about five of us... all from similar families (families might be defined as middle class in their communities) would save up our money and buy sweet potato pies as we walked home, and we would go home and play ball in the block. There were all kinds of things we did to entertain ourselves because we did not want to go into our houses. Those people (adults at home) had enough frustrations (little money, discrimination, and difficult personal relationships with spouses and loves, he reported) that we did know how to stay away until we had to go home... so we stayed in the street together, just talking and talking.

At first, part of what made the men's settings remembered as such warm and cherishing places were the spectrum of engagement opportunities for conviviality. On one end were youths who went to schools in their black communities. On the other, those who attended white schools. But from the men's reports, their convivial life took place within their own communities where they could concentrate on their concerns about both worlds in a stable hangout. At times, their choices of settings represented the steady mixture of alternative places made available to them over a wide range of different periods. It cannot be overstated because more than one group witnessed the inequality of their black communities. The majority of them reported they came from good families with parents who cared for them financially and emotionally. And they spoke of their parents or guardians as associating moral worth with academic achievement, and a belief in their son's value. In this respect, the men were additionally encouraged to socialize outside their family settings to further validate their self-identification and self worth (Ryan, 1994; Garmezy, 1991; Clarke, 1983). Certainly, they were able to go to their own people for acceptance and to strengthen their resolve. And I was struck by their right of domain and their desire to belong to a world that consistently informed them that they did not belong.

Then there was their ability, no matter what historical period they lived in, to have been granted considerable discretion to select the settings they interacted in even though their parents maintained considerable indirect control over their options.

Lastly, the data raised the possibility that a larger pattern existed which helped shape the men's social development through the dynamic interplay of the men's family, personality, and the places they chose. This general connection was found, no matter what age or what part of the country. Thus, I was led to believe that the men had more similarity of experiences than not.

In the next section, I examine in more detail, the types of settings the men used.

6.2   SETTING TYPES FURTHER EXPLORED

While no single setting the men used should be expected to have met all their needs, they did appear to offer varied benefits of service and opportunities in their variety. In this section we examine the distinctions.

They seemed to fill the specialized needs of young blacks which were fundamentally to help them master the competencies necessary for successful transitions to adulthood. And too, they established for them the needed connections to others. In all, each setting that the men described allowed them to learn and practice skills necessary to overcome obstacles youths such as they faced.

In his work, The substance of things hoped for (1995), Dr. Samuel Proctor, the celebrated Harlem minister, supports this point of view. He writes:

Promoting youth development requires attention. . . to the contexts in which learning and social interactions take place, and how these interactions are experienced by the adolescent. Engagement. . . connection of youth to self, peers, adults, group and community as both recipient and giver is prerequisite of competency development. Skill building is best achieved when young people are confident of their abilities, contacts and resources. This means that youth need to be nurtured, guided, empowered, and challenged by important work that they perceive as relevant. It means that they have to be engaged in constructive relationships with peers and adults.

Given this perspective, I examined in closer detail the types of settings the men used. Generally, settings could be described as three major types. They were (a) organized sports settings, (b) informal sports settings, and (c) organized youth program settings.

6.2.1 Organized Sports Settings

Of particular relevance were the organized school sponsored efforts. Eight of the 28 men said they were primarily involved in sports settings at school that included membership on a baseball, football, or basketball team. Generally, they all said they were the star players. Only 2 men played on racially mixed teams. The rest, on segregated school teams. Insights into the reasons most of the men joined school sponsored teams showed these reasons: (a) greater opportunities found for advanced competition, (b) resources of coaches to guide them to meet their needs, and (c) opportunity for leadership in a diverse program of sports, games, social, and outdoor recreation, special events, and other activities

One man, JW, described his experiences on his school basketball team in this way:

The coach of my school basketball team lived on the top floor of our house. So, I felt I couldn't get extra favors because he knew the family. It added an extra pressure but I tried to develop as a good player. I became "the most valuable player" and the team went out of town on 20 or 30 games in other towns. It was great and it exposed we blacks to a better life and really focused me.

6.2.2 Informal Sports Settings

Seven men used this type of activity which included informal play lots or a group or groups of neighborhood boys on a neighborhood playground, athletic playfield, pools, vacant lot, meeting spaces within schools or parks. These settings usually functioned without the interference of an adult coach or leader and were peer controlled.

SA, a 49 year-old banker, sat with me one afternoon in his office and told me about his experiences with his group of school friends.

There was no library in the town, no theater, and no movie. As a child, most of my recreation was in the form of athletics. When we got out of school we found our playtime because once you got home there was no more with chores and schoolwork. Within the three to five miles of our homes, we concocted a competition so that we could run track to our homes. The residents of town all knew us and what time we'd be running through to watch us. As we ran by we had to say hello, how are you. As young boys we were taking it serious because we didn't want to lose. There were ten of us and no matter who won or lost, the friendships survived.

From my discussions with these men and the other men in the profiles all spoke of their sports activities as very shaping, strengthening, and happy times. For them, sports and being on teams had an important impact. I suspected it had something to do with turning their unremarkable adolescent days into something heightened and exalted. Frey, in his work, The Last Shot, (1994) calls it "the rhythm of winning and losing and the dramatic first opportunity to take a long denied place in the mainstream of America." Thus, involvement in sports activities, whether formal or informal, could be seen as giving the men who were in possession of so little, materially their chance for a piece of the American dream through a scholarship for college, girls, status, pride in representing one's town, community, school, or to be sought after.

On the team they met kids like them at a critical juncture of their lives, adolescence. And in some ways, the men in sports and on formal teams received better attention than other kids in the high school from coaches who often acted as father figures. And I am reminded about BA, who spoke of the neighborhood he grew up in where baseball was the fabric of life there, and everyone followed the fortune of the young players. It suggests that for the men, sports and the process of playing was their version of the American dream. In a cruel parable, most of them began with little and slowly accrued success through hard work in a system designed to help those who helped themselves. And in hoping for the best, success was commonplace, but perpetuated by inequality.

6.2.3 Organized Youth Program Settings

Six men used this setting which included boys' clubs, PAL organizations, community centers, ROTC, and Naval Corps., and church youth settings. I learned that organized youth programs like these were developed to provide what Mincy in his work, <u>Nurturing Young black Males</u>, listed as critical components of places if they are to meet the needs of black male youths. They were (a) safety and structure, (b) belonging and membership, (c) self worth and an ability to contribute, (d) independence and control over one's life, (e) closeness and several good relationships, (f) competence and mastery and (g) self awareness and spirituality.

The men spoke often of these settings as safe alternatives to negative influences. Many of the men reported they provided a full range of athletic and social opportunities that were important for them. For instance, they learned how to appropriately use time and have the potential of adults to guide them in learning life skills and social competence. Also they were helped in reducing their adolescent feelings of anxiety and depression.

FK illustrates this view when he spoke of his Minisink Center experience.

Two or three times a week I went to my Minisink program. Because I was a junior leader, I put on my cadet uniform and went there. I was never much of an athlete but I played handball there. It was just that nobody in black neighborhoods played handball but I could there. We used to have 200 or 300 kids there and Minisink was the clubhouse where you learned to be community minded, gentlemen, and gain increasing roles of responsibility and leadership. We were proud to be there and we didn't want to let our leaders down.

6.2.4 Church programs

Of the 6 men who primarily used church settings, they did so because black churches have historically deep rooted roles as a stabilizing presence in black communities, and even more so with black parents. Historically, black churches have provided sanctuary and positive direction for their members. Most of the men reported they were sent to church settings by their parents and churches provided opportunities for them through leadership roles in youth ministries, choirs, usher boards, and peer group sessions. These church settings also offered the men opportunities for character development and culturally sensitive programs with opportunities to achieve, associations with the communities' human capital through positive adults and peers, and the opportunity to contribute to the community in a positive forum.

Mr. CC is an example as he replied: From the church we had a basketball team run by the men of the community and the church. We would travel to other places and play the surrounding towns, which gave the young men an opportunity to travel to other cities, and there was the choir we were on too. At one point in time, there were three of us from the choir playing on the same team but never on Sundays. Our church leader had gone to college and had three kids of his own. He challenged me more than anyone I ever met. He would save his papers or do research work when he knew I was coming and we'd sit on his porch and talk about world events, history, politics, whatever, and share and learn from one another. It was he that motivated me to want to go to college, which I shouldn't have because I didn't have any money.

In general, the lessons the men learned in church activities were in direct relationship to their hard work, personal pride and deep faith in a future filled with memory and purpose by their parents, church, community and themselves. Dr. Procter credits black peoples success to the "spiritual core found within them and the lessons learned at home and church from aunts, uncles, parents, grandparents, and neighbors." From he and the men the message was made clear in the church youth settings, "You are important and no man or woman will look down on you."

In the next section I examine in more detail how the men's used adult and peer controlled settings.

6.3 THE UTILIZATION AND ROLE OF SIGNIFICANT ADULTS AND PEERS IN THE SETTINGS

6.3.1 The Role of Adult Controlled Settings

Twenty-three of the 28 men reported they used adult controlled settings. The rest, 5 men, chose peer controlled settings. I found those who used adult controlled settings willingly subjected themselves to adults to shape them. They spoke of using their settings during the painful time of adolescent transition when they needed to develop their individual potentials. For many of them, this period led to apathy, pessimism, frustration, and hopelessness. If we accept that premise then we can argue that the men needed settings away from the influence of "negative street life" and as mechanisms for self-preservation. Mincy (1994) agreed, adding that community institutions have historically provided black youths with significant adult mentors to promote certain types of positive behavior. As such, the presence of role models and mechanisms of social control employed by adult mentors reproduced socially approved behavior in the settings. However, I did find variations of influence and opportunities from the adult mentors.

When I looked in detail at the life histories of the men, invariably the influence of one or more adult mentors seemed to strongly effect their adolescent maturation and direction. These adults influenced youths who were not their children and worked in sports programs, schools, youth clubs, centers, and churches. These adults, the men said instilled in them the values and motivation that they needed and they were partly responsible for their lives of meaning. It is significant that 23 of the 28 men (82%), came from low-income neighborhoods. And, too, that each with the exception of one man, had parents who worked hard to assure economic stability for their families. Most of them reported their families encouraged them to be strong and not taken for granted. In turn, their families were willing to allocate some of their training to settings in an effort to reinforce those teachings.

Without question, black male youths need the security of trusting that their advisors as "adult relievers" can make accurate assessments of them and have the skills to help them succeed. At times, what they and their parents looked for from adult providers was clarity, consistency, and clear evidence of concern. Thus, for these men, parenting became a collective community activity (Sampson and Lauritsen, 1993).

Black literature supports that the community "helper" networks the men spoke of take on the intense emotional character of family ties (McAdoo, 1978; Aschenberger, 1973; and Williams, 1995). As such, the men's developing resilience was then facilitated by the knowledge that they were not alone but linked through a series of relationships, mutual cooperation, and aid.

While there is little empirical evidence in the literature on adult controlled settings, these arguments heightened my call for more investigation on the informal helping the men found in their communities. By and large, I learned that the adult mentors perceived success within the men's settings came from their taking the time, and having the experience and positive outlook to create feelings of family in settings where youths could go and feel listened to. Also adult settings could offer the comprehensiveness, flexibility, and variety needed by the youths to expand.

I asked the men if they ever discussed important concerns with any of the adults at their settings and, if so, who and what exactly did those adults do for them. The adults most frequently described were teachers (12), then church leaders (7), and youth center staff (4). For the men, teachers were described as particularly instrumental in their lives but surprisingly, not for their traditional roles of teaching, but their assigned roles of supervising non-academic school activities such as band, orchestra, debate, chess, or a sports team. More importantly, these role models provided for them esteem building through (a) providing positive personalities as role models to make them feel special, (b) being outstanding in their efforts to assist and show consideration, (c) opening up new worlds to them, and (d) in believing and taking time with them.

In school environments certain teachers were remembered as showing considerable awareness about the complexity of the men's adolescent characters and had a sensitivity to their strengths and potential. Clearly, some provided the youths with an opportunity to master skills of strategic and broader planning to achieve higher outcomes, and motivated them by treating them with respect and consideration. Or, in some cases, set them up to prove themselves worthy. One man, KP, a gifted student from a racially segregated southern town illustrates this point as he remembered his black high school teacher who greeted him in class every morning with, "Hello, Mr. President." He mused, "It was then that I decided to become the first black president." Today, he is a law professor from a prestigious Ivy League school who advises presidents from African nations all over the world. Another man, SA, remembered the teacher who tutored him after class in his rural community. He recalled he first learned refinement from her on the afternoons that she served him tea on "real china and related colorful tales of her life abroad." It was then, he said, "I swore to myself that when I grew up, I would experience that other world she made me so aware of." Today, he is an educator who oversees the curriculum for a large urban school system in disadvantaged communities.

The second type of adult provider reported was found in the churches and youth centers that the men frequented. Seven men mentioned these adults. Church settings were remembered as meeting places, political arenas and links to the outside world (Hamilton, 1972). Adults in these settings provided social organization and structure. And, in these places the men learned leadership skills, exercised their administrative and organization skills, and came to be important. One man, JM, was a gifted youth from a home with an authoritarian, cold father who found his son lacking in every area. JM reported it was his church setting which provided a refuge from his father and a place to meet other kids. For him, his church setting became a major social event for him and, unlike home, he was seen as a leader, and he said, "a member of everything; the choir, usher board, and peer counseling." He excelled and was looked up to and he credited his church setting and adult leaders with maintaining and reinforcing his expectations about himself. He wanted me to know that he held those adults as part responsible for his becoming one of the few black Directors of Securities on Wall Street. What I found significant about adult controlled settings was that the men through caring adults in partnership with their parents were able to develop substitute kinship ties to help them in the protective process.

Other themes were revealed by men who remembered their important peer experiences. And Ladner (1971) reminded me that black children generally grow up in a society of peers who exert strong control over their lives throughout their adolescence.

6.3.2 The Role of Peer Controlled Settings

Sometimes the influences of peers can be a major factor in the adolescent's socialization process. The concept of peer group here refers specifically to a cluster of associates who knew one another and served as one of each other's source of reference or comparison. In discussing the peer groups, of course, the neighborhoods social composition through friendship patterns and choices of friends had a big effect. For the men, having significant age mate peer groups in the neighborhood or school with direct and dominant effect on their daily lives (Newman, 1982) tested their developing identities, evolving independence and emerging behaviors. These peer-controlled environments were reported as informal settings; clique clubs, sports teams, and neighborhood vacant lots, or places situated away from adult interference. For these men, friends were their source of learning things and feeling more comfortable, confident, and secure in situations that provoked their adolescent anxiety.

Five men used peer-controlled settings. It is significant that four of them came from one-parent families and defined themselves as "very poor." They remembered that for them, their focused relationships with male peers constituted their lives becoming attuned to how they should begin to relate to each other. Common for them were situations that facilitated the learning process of certain types of behavior such as developing social skills, and how to engage in and maintain friendships. They reported achieving the skills of social ability, popularity, and competence in peer friendships, without the constraints of adults with their own agendas. They found this helped them strengthen their traits of resilience.

The men spoke of two to five friends that they regularly interacted with. All, but one man, said they chose friends who were from a class above themselves and had solid two parent families. Interestingly, the five men, with the exception of one man, came from families where mothers were the sole wage earner and worked extensively out of the household, which left their sons caring for younger siblings. One example was RT who grew up in Harlem in a tenement with sole responsibility of care for his younger brothers until his mother came home from work. Although alone, he said he carefully picked his friends as he said:

We played in a vacant lot at the end of the block... I looked after my little brother as we waited for my mother to come home from work.... We were out there every day.... My friends were sharper (smarter) than I was and most of them had two parents. Sometimes, I would hang out at their house until their parents told me to go home because they had to do their homework. I kept trying in school but I was always slower than they.

In a different situation, another man, AG, reported about his fear of his domineering father. Unlike RT, he came from a two-parent home in the Harlem projects. Like RT, his role was to watch his little brother until his parents came home from work. As a gifted student, he, too, chose his friends from a higher social class than he, informing me that they met every afternoon in a secluded school setting. He explained.

We had our circle of friends who met in the back of the school auditorium and they were always happy to see me. I could identify with them although they were better off than my family but I was smart like them and they accepted me. I looked forward to meeting with them every day so we could talk about anything and everything.

I found it significant that the relationships of the men in peer controlled environments were different than those found in adult controlled environments. That is, peer settings were generally informal, peer dominated, and voluntary. These men's experiences confirmed Sampson and Groves' (1989) findings that correlated family disruption as a major predictor for use of unsupervised peer groups.

Central to my thinking was that for these men, peer settings were the logical family type to turn to. They helped the men learn new things, and feel more confident and secure about situations that provoked their anxiety. Thus, peer groups could almost be viewed as a type of socialization and solidarity unit for them. In them the men found a sense of gratification to share their joys, fears, surprises, and disappointments. And the settings provided them with the norms and sanctions which could not be brought about by a single adult parent alone (Sampson, 1992). But, I also suspected while peer settings offered them bonding, nurturing, and socialization they were not prepared to teach the needed achievement skills of positiveness, production, intellect, and leadership found in adult settings.

But, the peer environments provided exposure to other youths their own age away from single parents overburdened with other important matters, and they served as the tangible resources their parent was expected to provide. And more importantly, an alternate means of generating self esteem.

A consideration of the findings led me to agree with the theory that place supports are "embedded" in a causal network of social supports (Shinn, Lehmann, and Wong, 1984). And, as Ladner (1991) asserts, the the role of peers for black adolescents and, I believe, found in both adult and peer controlled settings, serves a somewhat different and broader function than for those of other cultures. Undoubtedly, their settings taught the men to be strong and not allow others to take them for granted. Inherent in this attitude was the assumption that they must not let their guard down. So, early on, self defense mechanisms leading to distrust of "outsiders" became ingrained in their attitude. Also the ability to establish and maintain friendships was an important component in withstanding stress. But out of these choices, whether adult or peer setting environments, certain basic convictions and attitudes undoubtedly influenced the men's goal directions. I suspect participation in settings offered the youths direct benefits related to an association with a body of nurturing individuals identified as useful to help the men withstand negative influences.

In the end, I found that the clearest distinction between the men's choices to use adult or peer controlled environments seemed linked to family obligations. As such, parental involvements led to attendance in more structured environments. In the cases of the 5 men who chose peer controlled environments, 4 men were segregated from formal group interactions because of having the obligation of care for younger siblings after school. They said that peer settings more easily enabled them to take their siblings who could tag along with them in unstructured or nearby places. The fifth man utilized his "place" during school and spent his after school hours babysitting his younger brother at home.

Whatever choice each man made, I began to suspect for most achievement was enhanced from the people in the settings that they used. For others, through accident or self-struggle and personality. But whatever the context, settings seemed more impacting when other various supports, family, self, and community were dynamically linked.

6.4 MEN'S REASONS FOR USING SETTINGS AND THE LESSONS THEY LEARNED THERE

The particular reasons that the men were attracted to their settings were explored in this section. They were asked to describe in detail exactly what they did at their settings, such as its most attractive features, or what brought them there, and to recall how using the settings changed their every day lives.

Central to my thinking was learning whether exposure to enriching settings promoted opportunities for self-direction and self-sufficiency. My thinking came from the literature which recognized that adolescence becomes the turning point and period of decision for young men's lifepath choices (Gibbs, 1984; Bly, 1990; Milton, 1983).

The men recounted various physical settings that defined their social life and were significant in their adolescent socialization process. Included were their homes, schools, and neighborhood settings. They emphasized that the main attraction for them at their nurturing settings was the focus on empowerment, critical thinking skills, purpose, and high expectations, Mincy (1994) in his work concurs as he observed that black male adolescents perceive that they have control over their outcomes when they engage in a combination of healthy activities which (a) create new opportunities, (b) teach strategies, (c) help acquire and practice skills and the confidence necessary for implementing goals and (d) provide rewards inducing achievement goals.

The men reported such opportunities were found in their formal settings such as schools, clubs, sports teams, and church youth activities. They also found them in informal settings like neighborhood play lots or special gathering places.

They identified five predominant attractions that the settings offered them. They were (a) an opportunity to meet people like them, (b) it opened up a new world, (c) a place to learn a new social network and structure, (d) a place for nurturing and (e) a place to give them an arena to prove themselves. In most cases, settings offered multiple attractions to each youth (See Table 18, Appendix 1).

6.4.1 Meet People Like Me

Twenty-one of the 28 men were attracted to places which offered opportunities for engaging relationships with highly skilled, determined, hardworking youths like themselves. They also reported that it was not uncommon to join their settings not so much because they were drawn to the rituals of the organization but because they wanted to master the skills of leadership, judgment, and self-confidence.

MB, a 44 year-old architect and graduate from Yale Law School, who grew up with his stepfather, mother, and siblings in a Brooklyn public housing project during the late 60's, illustrates these men. He spoke of his need to develop identity, character, and confidence and credited his three-year involvement with his nautical cadets setting for disadvantaged youths.

> ... the intent of the group was to provide training, military training to give adolescents the opportunity to learn about the Navy... we were given field jackets, manuals and we learned Spanish, it was a volunteer organization. It was absolutely intellectual from the aspect of going out and presenting yourself... it was good training on knowing how to present ourselves... it was very successful.

Another man, KM, a 46 year-old non-profit administrator who grew up in the slums of Baltimore during the same period, emphasized the importance of the bonding he formed with his black schoolmates who were gifted like him. He said:

> I didn't have any peer relationships in my neighborhood. My friends and I met in the school auditorium behind the stage every afternoon... there I saw people I knew and who liked me and they were gifted students like me. It made me feel good that they always seemed happy to see me.

To be sure, a third man, FK, 49, an only child of his laborer father and mother who was a domestic, grew up in a Harlem tenement and was gifted and attended school out of his Harlem community. As an adult, he went on to become a Colonel in the U.S. Army. He fondly recalled his after school attendance at the Harlem Minisink Youth Center, and his reaction to is as a second home:

> Minisink was my outside family... it was like a clubhouse and the rules required that you do well in school... it had very high standards and everybody was "special." Three of my best friends today were Minisinkers. One is a judge, the other a banker, and the third a politician... we had some good times there.

I began to suspect that each man's setting, in a way, validated for them that being different, academic, directed, questing, and not streetwise was all right.

6.4.2 Opened New Worlds

Sixteen men reported on the calm and protective environment that their settings provided and how it developed within them feelings of being safe and protected. they felt it then enabled them to move beyond the safety to new worlds. And their settings made them feel good about themselves too. One man, RT, a gregarious outgoing man, described his special setting, a vacant lot in his Harlem neighborhood. He concluded that it was his setting that bridged his connection from community to family. He also asserted that his experiences helped shape him to be the person he is today:

> ... the lot was an experience for about ten of us kids, a trial and error. It was a place to play. It was a place to get in trouble. You saw a lot of things in that lot... we would watch the men gamble... hear arguments, see evangelists, hear gospel singers, and watch salesmen try to sell clotheslines or gadgets... bordering on the lot were buildings and people would play music, call down and watch the kids from the block play. they were all there and we were a part of their family as we were friends together.

Another man, TB, 61, and the chief court reporter for a major city grew up in a brownstone in Harlem with his rather large extended family of aunts, cousins, and grandparents. He acknowledged that the people in his music setting inspired him to look beyond the boundaries of his community. He recalled the professional black couple who gave him his first exposure to the black middle class and got him interested in classical music. He paused, smiled, and said:

> They (the couple) put together a symphony orchestra... I would rehearse on Saturdays for hours with them. By the time I was 14, I was the only black kid playing the cello for the New York All-City Orchestra. We played Carnage hall... I knew that I was somebody and I followed the couple all around to concerts and chess clubs and plays...

In his view his orchestra experiences helped him have aspirations for the new world around him and shaped him logically.

I came to understand that the social and middle class status exposures that most adult controlled settings offered the men access to new directions, and opened up their experiences to a world of expanded opportunities. Also, the study raises the possibility that success rates were higher for youths involved in more structured, adult controlled settings such as Minisink, the Navy Cadet Corps, ROTC, and organized sports teams. That is because they had clearly defined goals and objectives to develop a team effort than peer settings which used more loosely structured, settings like neighborhood parks, vacant lots, or informal spaces.

6.4.3 Learned New Social Structures

Eleven men reported attractions to settings that allowed them to take risks and offered them, for the first time, empowerment in exchange for responsive action. For man, their settings taught them some of their most significant roles; to be black males, family members, and peer group members.

In such an environment, KP, a 54 year-old lawyer who grew up in the south, reflected that his setting, the swing band he was a member of with his brothers, taught him the inspiration, direction, and leadership skills he has today. He said:

> ... the band my brothers and I formed played every weekend when I was in high school... people would pay us to play in night clubs... it wasn't

performance, it wasn't entertainment, it was bonding and sharing and communication. And we thought we were music and we were the notes we sang. . . we were not separate and apart from the notes we sang.

FB, 67, and a businessman, like KP, saw his experiences in his community Boys' club as helpful in directing his life. He said:

I don't remember their form but if I had not spent more time at the boys' club, I probably would have been a juvenile delinquent. . . it was a deterrent against giving into criminal activities because it kept the amount of racial animosity down. Bridgeport, at that time was a very racist city. . . the club did not have that attitude. Hundreds of boys went there and I learned about sound structure and the rules for being a man in society.. . . That place was a source of information for maneuvering life. . .

6.4.4 Place For Nurturing

Eleven of the men credited their places with reinforcing the essential qualities of kindness, generosity, and responsibility. In them, they felt they could be listened to and respected. Nine of those men were reared in segregated communities, the rest, two men in racially mixed communities.

One man, DD, a 49 year-old minister of a youth church at one of the largest black churches in the country illustrates the men who lived in segregated communities within racially mixed neighborhoods. he attributed his racially mixed high school baseball team for giving him a sense of belonging and identification. He said:

I was the first black to make the team and I played every position. I was very proud of the fact I was on the team and they were very supportive of me.. . . They helped you, not only in your sports development, but in any other kind of development as a young man. they made you realize that you had unlimited potential. . .

Interestingly enough this same man reported he was the son of ministers. And being so, both parents required him to fully participate in his church's youth activities. He, too, credited the responsibilities and nurturing that he received there to giving him a sense of importance, and knowledge and trust to make good judgements. In his case both environments, Black and White, seemed to work together to reinforce his sense of who he was and what he could do.

Another man, a 38 year-old architect who grew up in a racially mixed public housing project and attended gifted classes in a school out of his neighborhood informed me of his experiences with his black classmates after school in this way:

We were in class together, a group of students in the college bound track. It was no matter that you lived uptown or downtown, we rode the bus together after class. It no longer became a function of where you lived but whom you were with. We'd get together to play baseball or punchball after class. It just felt like a natural extension of going to school and we stayed together for a few years, a group of like-minded black kids.

A third man, 52 year-old, JM, the Vice President of Securities for a large Wall Street firm who grew up in a segregated Harlem community reminisced about his community church youth group in this way:

... A lot of young people were there... you had a lot of exposure in all types of settings. I think in retrospect it helped me out later in life. The adult leaders there, they never talked down to you, you know, even though you were a kid... they seemed receptive to listening and doing what you said, you know, and giving positive feedback. And they were always reinforcing the fact that you can accomplish anything that you do... I think many of us needed to hear that.

When I asked JM why he felt this way, I learned about another painful dimension of his life which I came to understand was similar to the experiences of two other men. These men, like JM, had fathers who were domineering and not emotionally demonstrative. These fathers encouraged their sons to work hard and do well in school. But it seemed the nurturing that settings offered was not received at home. Thus, in some ways, for JM and other men, settings helped them to gain feelings of validation, respect, and dignity. And, while insulating them from racism, it also provided a haven from everyone who devalued them.

When I examined the findings, I was concerned as to whether the place for nurturing was more needed in communities that were segregated or in those racially mixed. In all, I concluded from the men's responses that it was needed in both environments. And, while no one pattern of development was experienced by the men, settings no matter what type, gave the men strength in varied patterns to fit their varied needs.

6.4.5 Place To Prove Themselves

All of the men informed me that their settings were places, which were willing to trust them and give them high visibility and acclaim. their responses reinforced the assertion that they were taught positive, hopeful, and bright futures. They credited their experiences to their beliefs that their settings allowed them to take a dual approach to their existence by (a) understanding their role in a society as black males and (b) by preparing them to function positively in the less accommodating larger white society.

As the men refined and developed their new identities, they began to identify with those around them. Thus, they gained a desire to be like the adult providers and/or peers whom they admired. Clearly, the interview responses substantiated the assertion of much of the literature (Sutton, 1972; Janovitz, 1952; Young, 1990). For the men did create mosaics of symbolic places within their communities. In them, they shared feelings and gained fraternity, loyalty, and identity. More fundamentally, most of them concluded that their individual settings taught them to set short and long term goals, dream, and work hard to achieve them.

Of particular importance was the men's acquisition of social capital from their contacts, identification and respect for the adults and peers in their settings. In mentioning their settings, whether school, church, or community center, they did not travel alone. Instead, they applied the group's positive standards, unique social forms, and "surrogate kinship" ties to move themselves forward.

I came to understand that the men went to their settings with individualized needs. Each seemed led by their own unique experiences and personalities in their preferences of settings. Each was able to personalize their space and use them, share experiences with peers and generate the deep-seated values of their groups which, in turn, shaped their attitudes. Group membership in itself offered the men security, self esteem, identity, and the connection they required (Dunier, 1992; Williams, 1995; Barker, 1968). In doing so, settings were able to function as behavioral laboratories and exhibit, not only spacial but also social properties.

The findings suggest that socialization can be a reciprocal affair in which each person may be stimulating others, and acting on settings as well as reactive at the same time (Jacobs and Spradlin, 1974). Certainly, by the time of adolescence, the men had come to terms with the realities of the outside world. All agreed that they no longer expected honor or acceptance from the world at large. In encounter after encounter, most said that they made peace with themselves through acceptance in their own separate worlds of high achievement. They spoke of not being circumvented by classism, racism, and stereotyping. In such a context, I noted that other youths subjected to the same blocked opportunities, who lived in the same type of communities did not achieve. And the men reported that some of their childhood friends who did not have havens from the negative influences of their environments did become delinquents. Given these futures and not wanting to follow suit, the men searched for significant social supports to assure them to some extent despite their color, social acceptance. Also, they looked to strengthen their resolve through their own separate worlds.

The findings also show that while the roles of family and even the role of the men's community life varied, their experiences of formal and informal social supports were constant and in most cases, a liberating force and source of refuge. Generations of black adolescents sought camaraderie, adventure, and an ever-widening social world of nurturing and competitiveness. The social boosts that their settings offered them made their journeys to adulthood fun, challenging and focused in its own unique way. They said that they learned that whatever they chose to do, they had to do it well.

So, the kind of person that each man considered himself to ultimately become was embodied in the relationships they developed from their image of self which they lived daily, and their perception of self worth that was derived from participation in their settings. These were the elements of their transition from adolescence to adulthood. In the next section, I examine how the men felt their behavior changed after using their settings.

7
HOW THE MEN FELT THEIR BEHAVIOR CHANGED AFTER USING THEIR SETTINGS

The literature acknowledges that behavior may become a function of group membership (Hyram, 1972). Consequently my research led me to believe that the men's individual settings acted as refuges for them, with support systems and places for intervention and control over conditions which affected them. In this section I examine perceived changes in behavior.

The men were asked what behavioral changes, if any, they experienced as a result of using their settings. All of them agreed that change occurred. However, their experiences varied. What became critical for me then was to identify what their settings provided them with that seemingly enabled them to circumvent their adolescent life stressors and affirm high achievement behavior as both inevitable and desirable.

I began by examining what roles they perceived their settings played in their changes of behavior. The settings they used were varied and either formal or informal, adult controlled or peer controlled, or places for sports, church, play, or just community arenas to gather. Not withstanding, these settings were able to provide the conviviality and caring the men sought.

Alternately they played a significant role in teaching them about bonding, self-direction, and inspiration. Of the two setting types offered, adult and peer controlled. What was gained from the more structured adult controlled settings were the role models, and adult leaders to introduce and reinforce new modes of behavior and show the youths the competitiveness required to succeed, a system to provide opportunities for the youths to gain leadership roles. What was gained from using the more informal peer settings were development of friendships, opportunities for leadership, and insulative havens to reinforce positive directions.

In the end, the men who used peer settings and had positive directed friends achieved change less dramatically than those who used adult controlled settings. Central to my thinking was that most of those who used peer settings came from single parent homes and had the responsibility for caring for younger siblings. This variable may have had some influence. But, the key to behavioral change for all of the men seemed to lie in their ability to accept certain basic convictions, have a positive direction, and exposure to expanded opportunities, no matter what setting type.

Four types of behavioral change were described. They were (a) developed a sense of self and the ability to become a change agent instead of being acted upon, (b) made aware of a new society and desired to be a part of it, (c) learned socialization and how to develop and accept friendships, and (d) recognized that the world had certain rules and authority and gained respect for them.

Table 3. BEHAVIORAL CHANGES PERCEIVED BY THE MEN

Types of Behavior	# Gained This	# Did Not
Developed a new sense of self to overcome obstacles and be a change agent	12	16
Opened up a new awareness of a society they wanted to be in	8	20
Gained new socialization and friendship skills	5	23
Recognized that the world had rules and gained respect for them	3	25

7.1 Developed A New Sense of Self

According to 12 of the men (43%), the tendency to develop a sense of self was equated with taking charge of their lives.

A favored response was illustrated by KP, who grew up in the south during the beginning of the Civil Rights Movement. KP presumed that his high school political action setting taught him to expect more of himself. He explained:

I thought they (adult leaders at the setting) knew everything and so I went from being a boy who had believed in equal justice to an agitator demanding my civil rights. . .

After listening to KP, I realized that he and the others instead of letting the negatives influences of their lives control them, used their settings as places to maintain their self direction and transformation.

Another man, FK, like KP recalled his transformation was significant. Influenced by their involvement with their settings, FK who later grew up to become a colonel in the army and spoke on an earlier occasion about the distress he felt from his experience of isolation at his white school, fondly remembered his adult controlled community center setting as responsible for reinforcing his self worth:

Minisink (youth center in Harlem) was my life and the beginning of my coming out. It was there that I became sure of who I was and what I wanted to be. It was there I learned to stand up in front of a group and give orders and teach people and be respected for it. . .

7.2 Opened Up Awareness of a Society They Wanted To Be In

Eight men (29%) reported that their settings opened up a new world and a new society for them which they decided they wanted to be a part of. Their awareness of a new world propelled them to larger horizons and a new society. At this point, TB who grew up in Harlem during the Depression illustrates this view of his adult controlled community orchestra group:

I wanted to emulate the professional black couple that headed my school orchestra. I felt I wanted to gain the same aspirations that they had. On the weekends, they would let me go all over the city with them because they rented rooms from my aunt... I was 14 and every Saturday we would go to some wonderful restaurant... it would cost so much. Then we would go to their chess club of which I became a member also. From their orchestra, I was selected to play violin with the All-City Orchestra and we played at Carnegie Hall once... it was a wonderful time with them and with them, my mind was opened up to other places that went beyond Harlem....

Another man, 67 year old FB, spoke of growing up in his Connecticut town with very few blacks during the 40's. He joined his town's adult controlled Boys' Club, he said, because he needed to find a way to close the racial gap he experienced. He explained in this way.

I went there because most of the educated and those who desired an education wanted something out of life. The members of the club were there because the town offered few other opportunities of equality for blacks. At least the club which had about 200 kids from all different sorts of backgrounds, showed little difference...

I was surprised that his way of getting the stamp of approval was by joining his multi-racial setting. But FB and his peers showed significant insight into their own separateness and the behavior they needed to acquire if they wanted to reconcile themselves to their self-imposed view of their own moral worth. And yet, as he talked he made a surprising revelation about another setting that he used in his own community which he attributed to molding his adolescent character. FB went on to say:

I started to go to the pool hall when I was 15 years old. I used it as a place of socialization and learned if you could make it there, you could make it through life. The pool hall taught us (he and three other boys) how to respect others, and maneuver life problems. While the men argued, drank, joked, and gambled they did so in a mannerly, respectable way. Men spoke about what they wanted to do and what had to be done to accomplish their goals. And the men acted as mentors to us. They taught us right from wrong and served as models for us on how to interact with our peers and men of our race and others.

On occasion celebrities such as sports entertainers would drop by. And the pool hall had every social level of men from the community from the cop to the teacher, the minister, to the number runner. From them all, we learned that men got where they were by hard work. So, we boys learned to carry ourselves as these men.

Men of the hall had tremendous respect for one another. Their life problems were discussed such as how the men interacted with their jobs. And the boys overheard it all. The hall also required discipline in that the men learned to be under control at all times. If they said the wrong thing, someone could get hurt. We also learned the process of things. men did not play at major tables until they earned their way up from shooting at back tables.

I came to understand that the pressure FB and his peers felt that was exerted from the pool hall and its men, helped steer and guide his life in a positive direction of hard work, respect and the orderly process of things. Coupled with the pool hall was the support of his family and his own success ambitions.

7.3 Gained New Socialization and Friendship Skills

For 5 men (18%) learning to socialize and accept friendships was the third major area of change. For MB, an impeccably dressed 40 year-old architect and lawyer, his setting, the nautical cadets, which he attended for three years, was remembered as the place where he learned to prove his worthiness and getting on the same track as similarly driven whites. He said:

> We learned all kinds of things about the navy and we were given filled jackets, manuals, and we learned Spanish. . . it was absolutely very intellectual in just about every aspect of being there and going out to present yourself. Our ties had to be just right. . . our shoes had to be shined, and we developed such camaraderie and closeness, it was like being in the military which shaped me to be more open. I could be an excellent student and it gave me a sense of value about my life.

For him, I'm sure unintentionally, but clearly implied, was learning how to socialize, develop, and accept friendships.

7.4 Recognized That The World Has Rules and Respected Them

As the men grew, learning and respecting the rules of the world and how to succeed became important. Three men (11%) spoke of this change. One man, DD, a minister for his church's youth congregation, who grew up in New Jersey and went to a predominately white school, attempted to comprehend his adult controlled high school basketball setting in this way:

> It showed me respect for authority and discipline and gave me self-discipline. I think actually it was the discipline that mattered. I had to respond and I had to live by the standards that were established. And, that was always good for me living in a structured environment. I know it impacts on one's character and it gave me a sense of order and value about my life.

RT who grew up in Harlem and was one of the 5 men who participated in peer controlled settings, was similarly affected as DD. He expressed his feelings about his adult controlled Catholic high school singing group in this way:

> I got the experience of discipline and understanding about the things I wanted out of life and how to go about getting them.

When I appeared puzzled, he went on to clarify his position for me:

> I had gone to public school at an early age and I was rebellious throughout high school. I found Catholic school strict and the nuns disciplinarians who gave you the ruler on the back of your hands. But it was a competitive environment and they took you outside the community to a bigger world that you had to deal with.

In all, the men acknowledged that support from community settings offered them an invincible quality. And for most adult controlled settings seemed to offer more direction and certainly more structure. And settings produced opportunities to develop the needed maturity and confidence which they needed.

The dominant view was that qualities such as positiveness, production, intellect, and social skills were reinforced more by adult settings. But, through their varied relationships and associations the men became like those they interacted with, and their transformations occurred. Thus for them, settings became the places that they rehearsed for life. They became their "finishing schools" where mutual responsibility, accountability and teamwork were reinforced, practiced, and imposed without danger to the men's self esteem.

The men gave strong evidence that many children and adults with similar backgrounds can and do overcome life's difficulties.

At this juncture, in my view, the men's outcomes served to build a sense that settings can be important in maintaining self-direction and thereby behavioral change. Moreover, the greater role of the men's settings was that they offered them the finite bounded regions that could generate the group's values to shape them (Barker, 1968; Hyram, 1972; Dunier, 1992). It is also significant that according to the men, these settings helped to create new balances for them by undoing old perceptions, reversing entrenched habits, and inculcating new behaviors and attitudes. In face of that, they were able to mold the men's youthful characters.

8 CONCLUSION

8.1 REVIEW OF THE RESEARCH PURPOSE AND OBJECTIVES

The purpose of the study was to explore the relationships between high achieving black men's lived experience from using adolescent settings in their black communities to their present outcomes.

Discrepancies and similarities between the men were identified and analyzed. Similarities among the narrative accounts indicated settings had specific attractions for the men and effectively influenced them. Differences in selection through elaboration of life events showed a creation of "place group identities" when change happened. Comparison of the men's accounts of same or similar setting experiences revealed descriptions tending to be repeated in a highly similar, although not identical form by some of the other men.

The study differs from previous research in that I attempted to examine in depth the components found in adolescent settings that produced support to black adolescent males and enhanced their sense of self-esteem, empowerment and self focus. Thus, the connections between the men and their settings were traced as I considered how each was able to find his own place culture, and contribute to them to in turn, be shaped by it.

The purpose of the research was not to study adolescents. Instead, it was a study of adults who looked back, perhaps at times somewhat selectively and not reflectively, on what happened to them in their settings and how their outcomes were influenced by it.

The defining theme of the dissertation was that black adolescent males from disadvantaged communities could be directed to adult high achievement through adolescent settings. What follows in the next section highlights and touches upon the main themes found in the body of the work.

8.2 SUMMARY OF FINDINGS

When I examined the recent works of black literature, they were a welcome departure from most of the literature on black families. These black works revealed the real diversity found in black families and communities, and documented the experiences of those who were poor, yet enjoyed a certain degree of abundance and privilege. Paralleling these findings, my own responses held a mixture of recognition as the research showed me glimpses of the middle class values that I knew and grew up with, and the people I interacted with in my daily life. I then knew that part of my anger in response to the distortions of black adolescents was a reaction to the dismissal in this country of those "poor" black adolescent males who consistently had middle class aspirations. In this context, I directed my research away from the usual focus on individuals and families to an examination of the environmental settings black male adolescents used within their communities to shape them to become high achieving adults.

The men revealed the nostalgia, ambivalence, and insecurity that often accompanied their ascendancy. Throughout, I was struck by the way their identities changed. In the end, I learned how the men's personalities, families, settings, larger communities, and historical context were woven together in their development. The men seemed confident that their community settings played a significant role in their purposeful paths to achievement. Hopefully, the finding that follows will give some insight as to how.

The findings were compiled over a year and are a sampling of black male high achievers' psychology. Largely my own work developed from reviewing literature on black men's stories such as The Cocaine Kids, Slim's Table, the Rage of the Privileged Class, and Nurturing Young black Males, to my own conversations with black men from a wide variety of professions and experiences. From my presentations of the men's stories, my research stance grew enormously from a simple focus on one cause such as settings as being responsible for the men's pursuit of high achievement, to a deeper understanding of the multi-faceted influences responsible and embedded within the diversity of the men's environments.

Throughout the year, the data took me on a historical journey examining the men's available patterns of support. I found that their individual experiences seemed to transcend their generational differences that spanned over 50 years. As I brought their stories forward to each succeeding generation, I found that theirs is a story with a common thread of hope and resilience. It offered data with implications for the under class argument. Also, it can be applied even to today's youths at a point when the social capital resources available to them now are more than ever before. That is attributed to the upward trend of gentrification occurring in disadvantaged communities by black and white middle class immigrants seeking a return to the traditional sense of community and caring.

What follows shows findings on the men's personalities, families, community life, the settings they used, attractions offered by the settings, and the effectiveness of the settings in changing the men's future aspirations.

8.2.1 Family Background

Most of the literature on black families reflects a minimization of the black fathers' presence in the home (Alston and Williams, 1982; Crockett, Egglebeen and Hawkins, 1993; McAdoo, 1988). From these perspectives, black families were represented as stereotypical single parent homes with black mothers plagued by the stresses of making a living thereby relinquishing the responsibilities of child care to others without providing for proper supervision. At the core of this thinking is that the departure of the mother leads to a weakening of the child's ability to protect himself against the environment (Lewison, 1935). Other researchers, Polokow (1933); Mulroy (1995); Garmezy (1986); and Wertlieb (1987) support the black child's ability to overcome parental losses through their experiences of other life events which can be long lasting. A very different impression emerges in the literature that depicts black mothers as the "driving force" behind their son's adult successes.

My findings are closer in view to works, which represent black families as the socialization unit and domain of the adolescent's greater personal involvement (Billingsly, 1988). Thus, the major role for black families becomes to fulfill the basic functions of protection from danger, provide material satisfaction, and integrate their sons into the mainstream of society. At times, parents' involvement and family relationships are seen as significant in shaping adolescent personalities and instilling modes of thought and appropriate behavior important for adult life (Mincy, 1994). Also to prepare them to combat the negative images and cultural stereotypes of the larger society (Leadbeater, 1996).

Similar to the literature by black scholars, the findings show a link between the men's parents' work socialization and their middle class perceptions and expectations of hard work and education for shaping their son's high values. The effects were great with 27 men (97%) reporting that they came from stable, work oriented family backgrounds where at least both or one of the caregivers were fully employed. Of those, 23 men (85%) came from two parent homes where both parents regularly interacted with them, encouraged high standards, and positive social orientations. For single parent homes (4 out of the 5 mothers), it seemed probably that they were socially overwhelmed and had fewer activities with their children than two parent households, and exerted less control over their sons free time.

The need for father figure male role models in the home for goal directed development seemed plausible. And in varying ways the men's fathers helped to shape them. The role of mothers as "driving forces" was shown to be limited with only 3 of the 28 mothers described that way.

Instead, partnerships of both parents seemed significant for real goal direction and the model for how each man wanted to be, with the exception of one man who wanted to be the opposite of what his family represented.

Most of the men who reported painful experiences of discrimination did not deter their parents' ability or willingness to exercise control over their activities to shape their positive goal direction. Thus, in the majority of cases, the simple affects of family involvement and their cohesion with the adequate social supports provided through community, school, church, or informal settings reinforced goal directed opportunities and became a plausible determinant in developing the men's positive outlooks.

8.2.2 Adolescent Neighborhoods

Clearly, neighborhood ecology is a recognized influence over black adolescent life. For better or worse, it occurs when settings provide, supervise and exert informal control over peer groups. Their goal is to provide an opportunity for collective socialization. The goal of the disadvantaged neighborhood is to offer the social interactions (social capital), peer influence and other social connections necessary for positive goal reinforcement in the adolescent's daily life. Over the past 25 years, the research literature (Baughman, 1972; Banks, 1978; Jablonsky, 1993) and Lefcourt, 1982) well documents the traditions and appropriate value orientations that black communities convey to black children to encourage achievement. In this respect, Bly (1978) in his work concurs that for the typical black child whether rural or urban, his experiences within his community will influence his development of self-esteem. Mincy (1994) adds that for the black adolescent, his self image emerges from the influences of his black communities' attitudes, behaviors, values, and lifestyles.

Throughout the research, I couldn't help but notice that having a sense of being safe, isolated, insulated, and comforted were perpetuated in most cases from family to neighborhood and became part of the social causal process. Thus the influencing network worked to direct the youths to their eventual high achievement lifepath. It is especially important that the influence of family and neighborhood on the men seemed to depend on the availability of an influencing network of family, peers, and caring adults for direction of the men's behavior and development.

My goal became to identify the neighborhood types that the men grew up in and used to define their unique constraints and/or opportunities. I understood early on that their neighborhoods provide the stage for settings to empower and impact on their developmental outcomes. The research revealed that although the men came from a variety of communities; rural and urban, northern and southern, segregated (60%) and integrated (40%) during varied historical periods, each community had a common thread of support within it that allowed each youth who tried, to seek success. Although defined as "disadvantaged," each community offered the youths a variety of collective support settings that exercised formal social control and supervision over them. The strength of these neighborhoods contributed to the youth's perceptions of them and provided refuges from the less nurturing places of their individual communities and the stereotyping larger society.

Certainly, these assertions suggest that by offering needed nurturing and supportive opportunities, settings can help black male adolescents validate and reinforce a positive sense of self-identity. In this respect, it is not surprising that for most of the men their neighborhoods acted much like extended families. Within this context the youths could be viewed as nestled within their families who, in turn, were nestled within the neighborhood.

8.2.3   Perceptions of Personality and Resilience

Contemporary literature on black adults presumes that certain traits are central to achievement. They are (a) to have self-affirmation and (b) a positive sense of self and self-pressure (Edwards and Polite, 1992; Johns, 1993; Staples, 1994; Ryan and Franklin, 1994). In black families literature, the essential patterns found for resilient children are (a) strong kinship bonds, (b) strong work orientation, (c) strong achievement orientation, (d) strong religious orientation (e) strong social skills with adults and other children, (f) strong problem solving in a reflective manner (g) strong self perception with a sense of power rather than powerlessness and, (h) goal directed behavior with a sense of obligation and preference for active educational pursuits (McAdoo, 1985), Hill, 1975).

The findings show a similar impression as the men reported themselves fitting within five dominant personality patterns. Most were competitive and enterprising (13 men). The rest, shy and quiet (six men), rebellious and questioning (4 men), socially cheery (4 men), and one man was dreamy and adventurous.

Education was an important means for the men's upward mobility. And the men reported that they, as well as their parents, peers, and adults in supportive settings, found education and occupational values significant influences for their adolescent career aspirations and achievements. Eighty-nine percent of the men had been academic achievers and of those, 68% were rated as gifted.

While the men's personalities varied considerably and the variance is understandable, their commonality was their own motivation and drive to survive. Successful mastery required that they use their own styles to work for them against the obstacles to their achievement. This suggests that the men fit the patterns defined as resilient. But while they seemed varied, they held critical connections between the individuals and the places that they used. Most of the men tried to fill the gaps in their lives and the needs of their personalities. But whatever their needs, they sought out places which filled them and, in turn, their individual characters played a role in their transformations by allowing them to be led to settings that were appropriate for them.

8.2.4 Racism

Racism and socioeconomic disadvantage often converged to impact negatively on the men's adolescent development. They were often confronted with extreme negative environmental stresses from existing in larger societies that offered them a perceived sense of social alienation and discrimination. Clearly, at any given moment the men observed these threats to their positive development. And, they reported that in spite of their intellects, they were aware that they were not treated as equitably as whites. Thus, to prove their worth they tried to excel in academics and sports. When that was not enough, they still realized the value of education and pursued it for their career aspirations. But implicit in their search was to find places where they could meet boys like themselves. Also, where they could feel safe, validated, cared for, and admired for their own drive. In turn, these supportive places offered them assistance to transcend racism instead of letting them be sunk by it.

8.2.5 Recollections of Settings That Most Strongly Influenced The Men

It is postulated by human geographers Tuan (1980), Ralph (1976, and Buttimer (1980) that a personal attachment to a geographically locatable place offers a person a sense of belonging and given purpose to his or her life. These assumptions suggest that settings or places could be considered as significant in providing a sense of rootedness in an adolescent's life.

The research suggests that communities offer black youths whose personalities and families predispose them opportunities to take advantage of the niches available for interaction, bonding, and goal direction.

The men used multiple settings (2.3) but each identified a major setting that had the greatest impact on what they became as adults. Use of settings regularly depended on the opportunities made available. Their choices of settings represent a steady mixture of the alternatives available within their communities. Those most frequently used were non school based sports groups (10), non school based social group settings (9), church youth center activities (8), school based choir, orchestra, and band (8), neighborhood playgrounds and play lots (8) community based youth centers (7), school based informal settings (6), school based sports teams (4), school based chess, political, or debate teams (4), and school (2).

Part of what made the men's settings important to them was that they offered the warmth and conviviality that the men sought. In this settings, I suspect the youths were able to concentrate on the remnants of a world that they sought for its material and personal opportunities. The significant idea revealed was that the world that they wished to belong to constantly manifested ways to inform them they did not belong. Clearly, this means it was the stability of their comforting settings, the challenges, learning, meeting and exposures, and interacting with different kinds of people including on sports teams and some school based settings, which reinforced the men's belief that they could belong. Settings also shaped their individual social developments to set the stage on how to achieve.

In regards to historical use differences the research revealed that no matter what historical period the type of settings the men used varied only slightly from generation to generation. The variation was found to be caused by the development of community center buildings in the 70's and 80's. Prior to these buildings types, the men used church buildings as youth centers from generation to generation. Afterwards, settings were chosen with considerable discretion and the men's parents maintained considerable indirect control over their options. It is well documented that in many cases although settings varied from place to place, they fit into the men's disadvantaged communities with a common mission. That was to provide enough supportive services to meet the needs and strengths of each adolescent and enable him to enjoy social and economic mobility. In general, the necessary component to effectively impact on the men was their ability to offer a variety of choices of settings to match the varied needs of each adolescent.

8.2.6 Reasons for Using Settings and What Actually Happened There

At the core of an individual's physical world, their past constitutes the places and spaces that instrumentally serve to satisfy their psychological, social and cultural needs. From these experiences emerge particular values, feelings, and beliefs about the physical world around us.

In equally compelling ways, Hyram (1972) and Barker (1969) describe such settings as environmental behavioral settings, which may include formal or informal groups (gangs), sports teams, church youth activities, or other forms of community youth opportunities. From Whytes' Street Corner Society (1943) and Walter Sullivan (1994) we focus on "partial communities" which lie within the larger communities. All these works conceptualized the idea for me as I came to understand that settings, as I had conceived them, could offer not only spatial but social opportunities for its users. In them, people could gather to perform certain duties at a specified time. Thus, in my thinking, the men's settings could be defined as associational niches that were organized, discovered, and cultivated by both parents and children. This impression was substantially the same as my research.

Within such contexts, it seemed that the settings the men described reconciled a need for support that each adolescent had in order to achieve. The settings' attractions were varied in that they (a) offered opportunities to meet new people, (b) opened up new worlds outside of the community, (c) gave new opportunities to learn different social and class structures, (d) offered nurturing, and (e) provided a place to have fun, learn new skills, share feelings, gain fraternity, loyalty, and a strong identity.

It is clear that the men quested for comrades, adventure, competitiveness and an ever-widening world of nurturing. These were the elements of their transition. The social boosts that their settings offered made their quests more focused in its own unique way and taught them how to do whatever they had to do well.

One feature that I found of particular importance was their acquisition of social capital along their journeys to achievement. This link evolved from their contacts, identification, and respect for the adults and peers that they interacted with within their settings.

In any case the adolescent relationships that they developed between image of self which they lived with daily, and their perception of self worth, which they derived from participation in settings, embodied the kind of man each considered himself to become.

8.2.7 Adult Controlled Settings

Outside of the home, the influence of community members upon the socialization of youths is often very strong. The research showed that the men benefited from their direct relationships with adults in settings. The works of Werner (1990) and Gabarino (1992) agree that the presence of "nurturing helpers" within the community are an important factor in the disadvantaged adolescents' search for the comfort, reassurance, and structure that they need.

The findings show that essentially 23 (82%) of the men used adult controlled settings which their parents sent them to. Adult providers in these settings reportedly gave the youths (a) role models with positive personalities and dignity, (b) made them feel that they were "special," (c) assisted and showed consideration of them, (d) opened up new worlds to them and made them aware of mores beyond their communities, and (e) took time with and believed in them.

8.2.8 Peer Controlled Settings

Not withstanding, the balance of 5 men (18%) used peer controlled environments located at neighborhood playgrounds, baseball, or basketball courts or in informal places such as in school or groups of kids gathering at specific locations. Of these men, all but one man came from a single parent family and had primary care responsibility for younger siblings after school. Generally, in those families, mothers were the primary care givers.

For the men, their choices of peer friendships centered on interacting with youths like themselves of the same or higher social class. The data reflects that 43% of the peers were of the same class and 39% were of a higher social class. No information was provided for 18% of the men. Peer relationships pointed to an ability to provide solidarity units where youths could share their joys, fears, surprises, and disappointments with peers.

The clearest distinction I found between the men's choice to use adult or peer controlled environments seemed linked to their family structure and obligations of caring for younger siblings. For the five youths from single parented families who chose peer controlled environments, three men were limited from using more formal settings due to the responsibility of caring for younger siblings who could not tag along to more structured settings. A fourth man, the next to the youngest sibling in the family, had two parents but also had responsibility of after school care of his younger brother. A fifth man had no siblings, but rebelled against a goal directed mother who tried to prevent him from interacting with neighborhood playmates.

The difference in the setting types seemed based in structure and mechanisms used. Adult controlled settings offered the historic community model found in black communities, and provided the youths with significant adult mentors and role models with varied mechanisms of social control. These nurturing men and women, the coaches, teachers, choir directors, and community center directors instilled in the boys positive values and motivations that they needed to become responsible and future directed. Wide-ranging exposures and involvement in athletics, education, socialization, often times outside the community and critical thinking and planning skills required to succeed in the outside world were taught.

Peer controlled settings were generally informal and comprised of neighborhood cliques of friends gathered at vacant lots, informal sports teams, and social clubs. The defining difference here was that they were free of adult interference. Thus, the youths, themselves, became the resources for learning things and feeling more confident and comfortable about themselves. Common for these situations were the learning of certain behaviors and how to engage in and maintain friendships without the constraints of adults with their own agendas.

Clearly, peer controlled settings were viewed as necessary but limited due to lack of adult guidance, socializing units, and wide ranging opportunities offered. But whatever choice was made, adult or peer settings, the data on the men's involvements showed each setting type acted as a family away from home with certain protective and insulative responsibilities. And each instilled in the men certain basic convictions and attitudes which undoubtedly influenced their positive directions.

8.2.9 Perceptions of Behavioral Change and Why Settings are Still Important to the Men

Central to the research was to determine if settings could influence character. Most social psychologists define social influence as synonymous with conformity and the ability of the majority of peers to induce conformity of one individual (Swingle, 1973).

Lewin's work (1936) was the more compelling argument for me in that he recognized the psychological influence environments have on the behavior and development of a child. It was extremely important in that all aspects of behavior, instinctive and voluntary, were found in some ways shaped by environment. It became clearer when I reviewed the work of Lefcourt (1982). He analyzed how one exerts control over his/her environment and becomes achievement oriented as one's self-image rises. Rohner and Edmonson (1964) add that for change to become functional and initiate a new way of thinking, definite mechanisms must be established.

These findings raised an important point for my research which is, can settings by providing association with others engender behavioral transformation and the common goal of higher outcomes for black male adolescents.

All of the men agreed that they experienced behavioral changes through using their community settings. Forty-two percent developed a sense of themselves. Twenty-nine percent found new worlds opened up to them and 18% learned how to socialize appropriately and make friends. The remaining 11% learned how to respect rules and more importantly, authority.

Alternately, all of the men disclosed that their settings played a significant role in teaching them about the importance of bonding, self-direction, and inspiration. And, too, they acknowledged that support from community settings offered them an invincible quality. This stemmed from their acquired maturity and the confidence that they attained from using their settings. The dominant view was that both adults and peers reinforced qualities within them, such as positiveness, production, intellect, and social skills.

In the end, these settings and the adults working there, and the peers the men interacted with through these developed places provided opportunities, nurturing supports and direction to undo old negative perceptions, reverse entrenched habits, and inculcate new behaviors and attitudes for high achievement. As such, the findings reveal that for black male adolescents, exposure to settings as socialization networks led to more positive adult outcomes. Indeed, the men credited their relationships with their communities and the men and women who helped them; the scout leaders, band directors, choir leaders, community leaders, coaches, and peers whom they were involved with as stabilizing in their lives. These "helpers" provided the men with positive models, which they tried to pattern their lives after. It seemed the men needed men and women like those in their communities and used them as social capital in the acknowledged roles of teaching, supporting, encouraging, and, in effect, socializing with parents on the men's responsibilities regarding work, family, the law and being productive citizens. More often than not, these men and women acted as surrogate fathers for some men, such as JHS and BA, or for the rest, as third parties to augment the relationship between parents.

I learned that the standard concept for black males of being carefree and non-responsible as adolescents was not the case. Even with family love, in most cases, parents were unable to provide total protection from racism and discrimination, perhaps because of their own vulnerability. Thus, this network of "others;" caring adults and peers in partnership with families found throughout from different times, communities, and people specifically became necessary to help wrap a protective cocoon around each man. As such, the men could return to these cocoons from the outside world or from the negative influences of their own communities, to be buffeted from those who did not value them. These interactions appeared synergistic and reflected that the cumulative effect of black men's social support systems in adolescence could tip youths upward bound.

8.2.10 Final Thoughts

The study attempts to introduce new evidence on how black men interpreted use of their settings and how their settings affected the dynamics of high achievement in their adulthood. Moreover, the study explores how they made them the men that they became by encouraging them to do well and showed them how to do so.

The general lessons of the results are clear in that the antecedents of achievement for the men related significantly to (a) the strengths and weaknesses of their families, (b) their neighborhoods, (c) adolescent settings, and (d), eventually themselves. In this way, being a member of their family, community and settings developed support resources for their partnership approaches that promoted a collaboration of reinforcing perspectives, to increase the men's chances for success. Given what I learned, these trends led me to expect that settings found within black communities and at schools where other settings were generated such as sports or quasi-military, or academic associations acted as significant "behavioral settings" for these adolescents.

A notable limitation of the present research is that it will require a much more reflective, long-term analysis of the positive aspects of black communities and the impact social settings have on adolescent black males. In doing so, we can develop a more balanced perspective on the impact social capital has on social class upward mobility in disadvantaged communities. Notably, I argue that black communities play a difficult and more significant role in the socialization process of adolescent black men and as they show male adolescents how to facilitate the social networks within their individual communities to advance the development of their self esteem and self direction.

In all, the findings suggest several different avenues for future research to try and gain a better understanding of the effects of these relationships. One may also say that the findings represent only part of the process of an even greater complexity. And different populations may generate some different results.

In many respects, high achieving black men and women have used alternate means to find their way out of inner city and rural black communities for generations. However, it is possible that additional research is needed to open new frames of inquiry and more carefully examine the resources and settings available. In turn, to compare those found to the resources found in other less distressed communities.

Hopefully, the men's voices can collectively be used as a resource of significant experiences to articulate how to prepare for high achievement, not how not to. Only then, I suggest can the ideologies that justify inequalities be fractured. It is clear that the men here spin images of what is possible in a world that both threatened and protected them.

8.3   LIMITS OF THE STUDY

The scope of the study was limited to some extent by a variety of factors beyond my control. The voluntary nature of the sample limited the results obtained. As in all voluntary samplings, there is the possibility of there being a difference between the participants who chose to take part in the study as opposed to those who did not.

The study was restricted geographically to black men who spent all or a major part of their adolescence in the United States, and nearly half of the participants grew up in the New York City region. Hence, the findings may not be generalizable to high achieving black men who grew up elsewhere or outside of United States culture.

Also, a relatively small snowball sampling was used, which could restrict any efforts to generalize the findings to a larger population. Too, the data gathered was from the men's recollections of settings that they used during adolescence. Their experiences are based on retrospective remembrances, and may have reflected more nostalgic, and changed memories than actual influences. I was clear about understanding the possibility.

And finally, there was much information collected from the original interview schedule in a variety of categories not used here. This included data on (a) descriptions of sibling relationships, (b) types of housing the men grew up in, (c) adolescent work experiences and relationship with employers, (d) choices made as adults to achieve their life path, and (e) the men's assesments on whether they felt they had achieved or not. I chose not to include these data to keep my research manageable and focused on the settings' impact on the men.

8.4 IMPLICATIONS FOR FUTURE RESEARCH

The negative effects of poverty and alienation are well known and have taken a toll on the development of many adolescents in today's black communities. For too long, too little has been known about the frequent cycle of people who escape from disadvantaged black communities (Mincy, 1994). My research exposes the ability of black communities to nurture its male adolescents in their development and empower them for productive adult lives.

I paint this stance, not necessarily to mean that a black youth's use of an adolescent setting will predict the degree or type of his change over a period of time. But, it is not unlikely to predict his later levels of functioning. And, too, they may be used to predict that group participation for black male youths is terribly important. In the aftermath, we may assume that we can begin to predict the lifepath projections of other cultures from the consequences of their various behaviors within certain settings. Any other questions of other inferences will require more study in detail.

The literature on adolescent resiliency suggests that the net affect of environmental forces on developmental outcomes depends on the relative balance of the environments' "risk factors" versus equivalent "resistance or protective factors" (Jessor, 1991; Rolf, 1990; Rutter, 1987; Werner and Smith, 1982). My research attempted to represent the internal factors that contributed to the adolescent's perceptions that their environmental settings were protective and supportive. In turn, I wanted to learn how settings influenced the men's sense of self-empowerment and motivation to achieve.

Undoubtedly, one of the reasons settings are so strongly able to influence youths is because they spend so much time there. Generally, with parents forced to leave their children in the hands of others, the settings described in the research conceivably could exercise more influence over behavior through the continuous, intense involvements experienced there.

The men's descriptions conveyed their understanding of the ways they came to interpret and negotiate their community places. Much of what I learned came from their experiences in their places. What emerged then was to a certain extent both conceptual and abstract.

In the research I tried to reconstruct the adolescent places within the men's lives. They spoke to me about their experiences of painful race and class discrimination in trying to achieve. I tried to relate how the web of their personalities, family, peers and community influences led them to their choice of settings (adult or peer controlled) and the relationships and learning that developed in that use.

I suggest the plausibility that the men's individual settings were nestled within different communities, regions, histories, and historical moments, but were able to form throughout patterns of experiences that yielded resilient personalities and personal choices with a common goal of adult achievement.

My research exposes that settings may be varied, and either informal or formal, adult controlled, or peer controlled. We need to imagine a context in which such settings would be useful not only for "resilient" black male adolescents and families but also for youths who have less personal strength and more dysfunctional families but share the common threat of adult failure.

I hope my findings will display a set of possibilities to generate further studies on the opportunities that communities of color offer. In the sociological and psychological perspective, they shed light on the diversity of black communities, and have implications for the underclass argument. Hopefully, it reveals the interconnectedness of black communities and how they work in all their strengths as well as weaknesses. And, too, perhaps for the first time, how black families, community members, and youths act in concert to increase the black male youths chances for achievement.

I end as Dr. Proctor so eloquently reminds us. "We must reach back and find ways to help others come along, or the whole nation may sink."

I'd like to think of the research as a beginning that will sensitize psychologists, sociologists, and others to these issues. Subsequently, to look at the complexities of Black male identity from a more balanced perspective.

APPENDIX 1

DEMOGRAPHICS

Table 4. AGE DISTRIBUTION

Ages	#	% rounded off
28-38	5	18
39 - 48	7	25
50 - 60	10	36
61 - 70	4	14
71 - 77	2	7
Total	28	100%

Table 5. PROFESSIONAL ATTAINMENT

	Number
Church administrator	1
Lawyer	2
Architect	2
Pastor	2
Securities vice president Wall street firm	1
Securities director	1
Politics/chief of staff/legislative aide	2
Businessman	5
Real estate developer	1
Army colonel	1
Chief court administrator	1
Bank manager	1
Not-for-profit director	1
Building manager	1
District school superintendent	1
Psychologist	2
Community Relations specialist	1
Electrical Engineer	1
Total	28

Table 6. INCOME DISTRIBUTION

	Number	% rounded off
$30 - 39,000	1	3
$40 - 59,000	8	29
$60 - 79,000	5	18
$80 - 900,000	5	18
$100,000+	9	32
Total	28	100%

Table 7. EDUCATIONAL ATTAINMENT

	Number	% rounded off
High School	4	14
2-3 years college	5	18
4 yrs. college	7	25
Masters Degree	5	18
Professional degree (law, architect, psychology)	7	25
Total	28	100%

Table 8. CURRENT MARITAL STATUS

	Number	% rounded off
Married	18	64
Single	7	25
Divorced	2	7
Widowed	1	4
Total	28	100%

Table 9. ADOLESCENT NEIGHBORHOOD TYPES

Type Resided There	# Men
Northern Urban, Racially Mixed	6
Southern Urban, Racially Mixed	2
Northern Urban Segregated	8
Southern Urban Segregated	2
Southern Small Town Racially Mixed	3
Southern Small Town Segregated	5
Rural Other/Guyana	2
Total	28

Table 10. ADOLESCENT NEIGHBORHOOD LOCATIONS

	Number	% rounded off
New York City		
Bronx	2	7
Brooklyn	1	4
Manhattan (Upper Westside)	1	4
Harlem	9	29
Long Island	1	4
Total	14	48%
Northern States		
Connecticut	1	4
New Jersey	1	4
Kansas	1	4
Wisconsin	1	4
Total	4	16%
Southern States		
Georgia	1	4
Louisiana	1	4
Maryland	2	7
Mississippi	1	4
North Carolina	1	4
Virginia	2	7
Total	8	30%
Other		
Guyana	2	6%

Table 11. NEIGHBORHOOD TYPES BY AGE OF PARTICIPANTS

	Racially Mixed		Segregated	
NORTHERN	Urban	Small	Urban	Small
	29, 34, 38, 43, 44	43, 56, 67	29, 49, 50, 50, 50, 52, 60, 61	
Totals	5	3	8	8
SOUTHERN	45, 46, 51		49, 65	53, 54, 65, 72, 77
Totals	3	0	2	5
OTHER			38, 49	
	0	0	2	0
TOTALS	Racially Mixed 11		Segregated 17	

Table 12. HOUSEHOLD COMPOSITION BY LOCATION AND AGE OF PARTICIPANTS

	Racially Mixed Urban Father/Mother HH	Single Parent HH or Other Rel.	Small Father/Mother HH	Single Parent HH or Other Rel.	Segregated Urban Father/Mother HH	Single Parent HH or Other Rel.	Small Father/Mother HH	Single Parent HH or Other Rel.
NORTHERN	38, 43, 44	29, 34	43, 56, 67		49, 50, 50, 60	52, 61		
Totals	3	2	3	0	4	2	0	0
SOUTHERN	45, 51	46			49, 51		53, 54, 65, 72	77
Totals	2	1	0	0	2	0	4	1
OTHER					38, 49			
Totals					2			
TOTALS	Racially Mixed (F/M HH)		Racially Mixed (Single Parent, etc.)		Segregated (F/M HH)		Segregated (Single Parent, etc.)	

**Two men reared in northern, urban segregated communities *; (1) by his grandparents, the other by loving foster parents.

Table 13. MEN'S PERCEPTIONS OF THEIR PREDOMINANT ADOLESCENT CHARACTERS BY RESIDENCE AND AGE

	Northern Home Communities From New York City	Other	Southern Home Communities
Shy/Quiet	34, 38, 44, 50, 51		65
Totals	5	0	1
Competitive	28, 45, 49, 50, 50, 60, 61	38, 43, 49, 56	51, 67, 72, 77
Totals	7	4	4
Rebellious	29		46, 49, 65
Totals	1	0	3
Cheery			52, 52
Totals	0	0	2
Dreamer	52		
Totals	1	0	0

Table 14. FATHER'S PROFESSIONAL ATTAINMENT

Fathers	#
Dry Cleaners	2
Farmers	2
Barbers	2
Truck Drivers	3
Park or Wash Cars	2
Store Clerk or Garment District	2
Factory Worker	2
Subway Motorman	1
Carpenter	1
Salesman	1
Police Officer	1
Dietician	1
College Professor	1
Engineer	1
Pastor	1
Unknown/Deceased or out of house	4
Total	28

Table 15. MOTHER'S PROFESSIONAL ATTAINMENT

Mothers	#
Draper/seamstress garment district	2
Housewife	10
Farmer	1
Beautician	1
Court Clerk	1
Domestic	6
Teacher	3
Realtor	1
Pastor	1
Dietician	1
On public assistance	1
Total	28

Table 16. FATHER TYPES

Fathers	Number
Stable workaholic, close to son and role model	17
Low work capability but loving care givers "dawdlers"	3
Hardworking authoritarian - not warm or close to son	3
Out of home by divorce, death or abandonment	5
Total	28

Table 17. MOTHER TYPES

	Number
Loving Taskmaster - very involved with son's future	7
Low key and loving involvement in partnership with her husband	18
Not involved and busy	3
total	28

Table 18. MEN'S SELF PERCEPTION OF THEIR ADOLESCENT PERSONALITIES

	Shy/quiet	Competitive/ enterprising	Rebellious/ questioning	Socially cheery	Adventurer dreamer
GM		X			
FB		X			
CC			X		
JHS			X		
FK		X			
RC	X				
TB		X			
KP				X	
WB	X				
MB	X				
JW				X	
JM		X			
DD		X			
RT					X
PD	X				
SA		X			
WAC		X			
JH		X			
CM			X		
LH		X			
RM	X				
MK		X			
KM			X		
RG	X				
BB		X			
TC		X			
JC		X			
JJ		X			

Table 19. MULTIPLE SETTINGS USED BY THE YOUTHS

Settings Used	# Youths Used It	# Youths Did Not
Non-school based sports group	10	18
Non-school based social setting	9	19
Church/Youth center activities	8	20
School based band, choir, orchestra	8	20
Neighborhood playground, play lot	8	20
Community-based youth center	7	21
School based informal setting	6	22
School based sports team	4	24
School based chess, debate or political club	4	24
School	2	26

Table 20. FAVORITE SETTINGS USED

Setting Types	# Men Used It
Organized Sports Settings (school, church, or community sponsored)	8
Informal Sports Settings (neighborhood parks or racetracks)	2
Organized Youth Program Settings (ROTC, Naval Cadets, Minisink, Orchestra, Boys' Club, Community Center, Boy Scouts)	6
Church Youth Programs	6
School based Debate Club	1
Peer Cliques Informal Setting (music combo, meetings with friends in special places	5
Total	28

Table 21. WHAT ATTRACTIONS SETTINGS OFFERED

	# Youths Using	# Not Using
Meet people like me	21	7
Opened new worlds	16	12
Learned new social structures	11	17
Place for nurturing	11	17
Place to prove themselves	11	17

Table 22. ADOLESCENT SOCIAL CLASS OF FRIENDS

Same class	12
Higher class	11
No information	5
Total	28

Table 23. FRIENDS ADULT OUTCOMES

	# Prospered
Yes	25
No	1
Somewhat	2
Total	28

Table 24. MEN'S FEELINGS ABOUT SPECIFIC PLACES

	# Yes	# No
Gave them social network and structure	28	0
Gave important bonding	19	9
Gave direction and inspiration	13	15
Gave a value system and structure	9	21

Table 25. BEHAVIORAL CHANGES PERCEIVED BY THE MEN

Types of Behavior	# Gained This	# Did Not
Developed a new sense of self to overcome obstacles and be a change agent	12	16
Opened up a new awareness of a society they wanted to be in	8	20
Gained new socialization and friendship skills	5	23
Recognized that the world had rules and gained respect for them	3	25

APPENDIX 2

FOCUS GROUP INSTRUMENTS

DRAFT COVER LETTER FOR SURVEY QUESTIONNAIRE

March 28, 1996

Dear Sir:

Very little is known about the interrelationship between the Black male adolescent's use of group settings within his Black community and his subsequent goal directed behavior for high achievement as an adult?

I am currently conducting a research project that will examine the role, if any, that specific community settings play in the Black adolescent's adult success life path. That is, could these settings mold the Black male adolescent's norms to develop "potentiality" for his adult success? While Black men's stories are not the same, there may be many shared themes and outcomes.

My study is performed as a partial fulfillment of the requirement for my Ph.D. in psychology at the City University Graduate Center. Hopefully, it will offer insight into the opportunities for motivation that Black communities provide and help me document Black men's understanding of the role their African-American community settings played in motivating or discouraging their adolescent drive to achieve. The purpose is to be able to make policy recommendations for support of these positive, support settings for today's youth.

As an interviewee, you will be asked to discuss your recollections, experiences and opinions about important growing up places within your adolescent African-American community that will take approximately 90 minutes.

Participation is strictly voluntary. All information gathered will be confidential and used for research purposes only. And, data from questionnaires will be anonymous.

If you are willing to participate on this topic as an interviewee, your prompt reply will be greatly appreciated. Please return this form by mail in the return envelope to Sandra Griffin (address omitted), or call (number omitted) to leave a message; or fax your reply to (number omitted). Please write your name and phone number for contact.

Interviews are scheduled to begin within the months of April and May 1996 at a designated meeting place. I urge you to work with me and feel your involvement will make a difference.

Refreshments will be available.

Thank you for your assistance.

Sandra Taylor Griffin

FOCUS GROUP DISCUSSION QUESTIONS

Looking back over your life, were there community organizations (sport team, youth center, clubhouse, church youth organization) of which you were a member during your adolescence?

Could you list them?

Could you recall which of these organizations most strongly influenced you?

What organization was that? When? Why?

What usually happened in this organization?

Where was it located?

How would you describe how you feel about this place?

Were your experiences good? Why?

Why did this organization mean a lot to you? What made it important to you?

Who else was there?

What kinds of things did you do at this place?

How many (years, months) did you attend this place?

Why is this place still important to you? What did you learn from this place?

APPENDIX 3

PARTICIPANT INSTRUMENTS

Cover Letter for Recruitment of Participants

Date:

Dear Sir:

I am an African-American doctoral student working on my dissertation study. You have been recommended as a successful Black man and I am asking for your assistance. I am currently conducting a research project on how using certain community settings impact on the adolescent's successful adult life path.

My study is performed as a partial fulfillment of the requirement for my Ph.D. in psychology at the City University Graduate Center. While Black men's stories are not the same, there may be shared themes and outcomes between your experiences and those of other successful men. The purpose is to be able to make policy recommendations for support of these social support places for today's youths.

I am looking for high achieving men between the ages of 35-65 years old. As a participant, you will be asked to discuss your recollections, experiences and opinions about important growing up places within your African American adolescent community that will take approximately 90 minutes. I hope to develop insights into the role of the African American community in motivating or discouraging adolescents in their drive to achieve.

Participation is strictly voluntary. All information gathered would be confidential and used for research purposes only. And, data from questionnaires will be anonymous.

If you are willing to participate on this topic as an interviewee, your prompt reply will be greatly appreciated. Please return this form by mail in the return envelope to Sandra Griffin, 423 West 144th Street, New York, NY 10031; or CALL (212) 368-4677 to leave a message; or FAX your reply to (212) 866-6354. Please write your name and phone number for contact.

Interviews are scheduled to begin through the months of June and July 1996 at a designated meeting place. I urge you to work with me and feel your involvement will make a difference.

Refreshments will be available.

Thank you for your assistance.

Sandra Taylor Griffin

Interviewee's Introduction Script

The idea of the study is to find out how Black men grew up and whether their being exposed to adolescent places in their African-American communities had any effect, if any. It's the kind of information that nobody except those who went through it has.

What I'm doing is talking to people like you because it is important for others, especially African American adolescent males to understand as well as they can. So, I'm going to ask you to help me to tell your story. And, that's what I'm doing.

Here is a consent form for you to read. It describes the study, and if it's okay with you, sign one copy and let me have it. You keep the other.

I will be taping if it's all right. Nobody will be listening to the tapes except for the people of the project.

Adolescent Community Influence on Achieving Black Men

QUESTIONNAIRE

NOW, I'D LIKE TO TRY TO UNDERSTAND THE EFFECT YOUR ADOLESCENT COMMUNITY HAD ON YOUR ADULT ACHIEVEMENT.
WE NEED TO ASK SOME QUESTIONS ABOUT YOUR ADOLESCENT LIFE EXPERIENCES. THE INTERVIEW SHOULD ONLY LAST ABOUT 90 MINUTES.

I'D LIKE TO BEGIN BY ASKING A FEW QUESTIONS ABOUT YOUR ADOLESCENT FAMILY SITUATION. COULD YOU THINK ABOUT WHEN YOU WERE AN ADOLESCENT? (14-17 YEARS OLD)

A: **Adolescent Family Experiences: Questions 1 - 6)**

1. Tell me about your family: How many people lived in your family including yourself?

2. Did you have siblings? Yes ___ No ___
   How many sisters? ___ brothers? ___
   Where did you rank? (oldest, middle, youngest) ___

3. Did you live in?
   a) a private house ___ b) an apartment ___
   c) public housing ___ d) other ___

4. What was your parents or caretakers source of income? (Check all that apply)
   a) job ___ b) pension ___ c) SSI ___
   d) public other ___ e) other ___
   What was their profession?
   Mother ___ Father ___ Other ___

5. Would you describe your family's economic status as:
   a) wealthy ___   b) upper-middle class ___
   c) middle class ___   d) lower-middle class ___
   e) poor ___   f) very poor ___

6. Could you describe your relationship with your family while an adolescent?

NOW I'D LIKE TO ASK SOME QUESTIONS ABOUT YOUR COMMUNITY AND THE SETTINGS YOU USED.

B: **Adolescent Community Setting Memories: (Questions 7-12)**

7. Could you describe the community you spent your adolescent years? How satisfied were you with it? What were its worst aspects? Explain.

8. Do you remember how you spent your days? Could you walk me through a particular weekday? A weekend? Were there places you went to where you met with a group? Where did you go? Explain.

9. What were the feelings you had when you went to your community place? What was it like?

10. What exactly did you do at the community setting? How often did you go there? Who else was there? What were the most attractive aspects of it? How was your everyday life changed?

11. Did you ever discuss important concerns with any one of the people at the community setting? With whom? Tell me about that person. What exactly did they do for you?

12. Could you describe yourself as an adolescent? Do you feel you made any changes in your behavior or character after attending the community setting? How were your feelings and experiences there different than other places? Explain.

NOW I'D LIKE TO ASK SOME MORE SPECIFIC QUESTIONS ABOUT YOU AND YOUR FRIENDS' ADOLESCENT CHARACTER DEVELOPMENT.

C: Adolescent: (Questions 13 - 16)

13. Tell me about your school life. Tell me about your relationships with teachers and friends.

14. Did you work as an adolescent? What exactly did you do? Explain.

15. Tell me about your relationship with your employer and co-workers. Tell me how you used your earnings.

16. What about your adolescent friends? What were they like? What kinds of things did you do together? Where did you go? What happened to them as adults? Explain.

NOW, I'D LIKE TO KNOW A LITTLE BIT ABOUT YOUR ADULT EXPERIENCES.

D: Insights: (Questions 17 - 18)

17. Looking back, so you feel there were specific places that were helpful in your life path? Anything else?

18. When did you decide on your current career path? What choices did you make to get where you are today? Do you feel you achieved what you wanted to? Explain.

BEFORE WE END, WE JUST NEED TO KNOW A LITTLE MORE ABOUT YOU. THESE QUESTIONS ARE SOMEWHAT PERSONAL BUT, ALL YOUR ANSWERS WILL BE KEPT CONFIDENTIAL.

E: Bio-Data (Questions 19 - 27)

19.   Where do you live now? (Borough) _____

20.   What is your profession? _____

21.   Are you currently employed? Yes ___ No ___

22.   How much would you say you earned this year? Is it between?
    a) Less than $20,000   e) $60 - $79,000 ___
    b) $20 - $29,000 ___   f) $80 - $99,000 ___
    c) $30 - $39,000 ___   g) $100 or above ___
    d) $40 - $59,000 ___   h) Decline to answer ___

23.   How would you describe your present living arrangement? Are you?
    a) married ___   b) divorced ___   c) single ___
    d) living with a partner ___   never married ___

24.   Do you have children? Yes ___ No ___
    If yes, how many? _____ What are they doing now?
    _____
    _____

25.   Did you graduate from high school? Yes ___   No ___
    Year graduated: _____
    private ___   parochial ___   public ___

26.   Did you attend college? Yes ___ No ___
    Year graduated: _____
    What was your major? _____
    What degree did you attain? _____

    If you did not complete college, how many years did you complete?
_____

27.   What is your age? _____

    Thank you, I'm grateful for the time you spent with me. Of course, in case you have something else to say about this topic, you can call me. And, may I call you if I need further information regarding a particular area?

    Before you go, do you know anybody else I should talk to? Thank you very much.

BIBLIOGRAPHY

Ahlbrandt, Roger S. (1984). Neighborhoods, people and community. New York: Plenum Press.

Ahlbrandt, Roger S. (1986). Using research to build stronger neighborhoods: A study of Pittsburgh neighborhoods. In Ralph B. Taylor's Urban neighborhoods: Research and policy. New York: Praeger Press.

Allen, Walter (1986). Black American families 1965-1984: A classified selectively annotated bibliography. New York: Greenwood Press.

Anderson, Elijah. (1978). A place on the corner. Chicago: Chicago University Press.

Archer, Jennifer (1994). Achievement goals as a measure of motivation in university students. Contemporary Educational Psychology, 19, 431-446.

Barnes, Edward J. (1996). The black community as the source of positive self-concept for black children: A theoretical perspective. Social Problems, 43(3), 107-123.

Baughman, Earl E. (1971). Black Americans: A psychological analysis. New York: Academic Press.

Berry, Gordon Lavern and Asamen, Joy Keiko (Eds.) (1989). Black students: Psychological issues and academic achievement. Newbury Park, London: Sage Publications.

Billingsley, Andrew. (1988). Black families in White America. New York: Simon & Shuster, Inc.

Billson, Janet M. (1996). Pathways to manhood: Young black males struggle for identity. New York: Transaction Publishers.

Bly, R. (1990). Iron John: A book about men. Reading, MA: Addison Wesley Publishers.

Bronfenbrenner, U. (1979). The ecology of human development: Experiments by nature and design. Cambridge, MA: Harvard University Press.

Bronfenbrenner, U. (1977). Toward an experimental ecology of human development. American Psychologist, 32, 513-531.

Burns, Ken. Black youths facing crisis. (December 4, 1993). The Times Herald Record; (pp. 33).

.Caliver, Ambrose (1970). A background study of Negro college students. (Reprint 1933 edition). Westport, Connecticut: Negro Universities Press.

Clark, Kenneth B. (1967). Dark ghetto: Dilemmas of social power. NY: Harper & Row Publishers.

Clarke, Brenda A. (1987). Stress in black Americans. Dissertation submitted to the Graduate Faculty in Psychology.

Clarke, Reginald (1983). Family life and school achievement: Why poor black children succeed or fail. Chicago and London: The University of Chicago Press.

Cohen, M. I. (1979). The urban adolescent's interface with his environment: Health and meaningful survival. In W. Michelson (Eds.). The child in the city: Today and tomorrow, (pp. 193-203). Toronto: University of Toronto Press.

Cohn, Michael & Saegert, Susan (1985). Teenager's experiences of the environment at Phipps Plaza South. Study for Phipps Houses, December 1985.

Coleman, J. S. (1974). Youth: Transition to adulthood. Chicago: University of Chicago Press.

Coleman, James S. (1988). Social capital in the creation of human capital. American Journal of Sociology, 94 S95-S120.

Comer, James P. (1972). Beyond black and white. New York: Quadrangle Books.

Corcoran, Mary & Adams, Terry (1993). Underclass neighborhoods and intergenerational poverty and dependency. Report for the Rockefeller Foundation, June 1993.

Cose, Ellis. (July 11, 1994). "Caught between two worlds". Newsweek, pp. 28.

Cose, Ellis. (1993). The rage of a priviledged class: Why are middle-class blacks angry? Why should America care? USA: Harper Collins.

Costes-Kurtz, Beth E. (1994). Self concept, attributional benefits, and school achievement: A longitudinal analysis. Contemporary Educational Psychology, 19, 199-216.

Crane, Jonathan (1991). The epidemic theory of ghettos and neighborhood effects on dropping out and teenage childbearing. American Journal of Sociology, 96, (5), Pp. 1227-1257.

Csikszentmihalyi, M. & Larson, R. (1984). Being adolescent: Conflict and growth in the teenage years. New York: Basic Books.

Cuber, John F. & Kenkel, William F. (1954). Social stratification in the United States. NY: Appleton-Century Crofts, Inc.

Damon, W. (1983). Social and personality development: Infancy through adolescence. New York: W. W. Norton.

David, Jay (Ed.) (1992) reprint. Growing up black. New York: Avon Books.

Deutsch, Martin (1967). The disadvantaged child: Studies of the social environment and the learning process. New York, London: Basic Books Inc..

Downs, Anthony. (1977). The role of neighborhoods in the mature metropolis. St. Louis: St. Louis Symposium.

Dugger, Celia W. (1994). A boy in search of respect discovers how to kill: clues to the growing trend of violence among the young. The New York Times, May 15, 194.

Duneier, Mitchell. (1992). Slims table: race, respectability and masculinity. Chicago: University of Chicago Press.

Edelman, Marian Wright. (1993). The measure of our success. USA: Harper Collins.

Edwards, Audrey & Polite, Craig. (1992). Children of the dream: The psychology of black success. New York: Anchor Books, Doubleday.

Elder, G. H., Jr. (1980). Adolescence in historical perspective. In J. Adelson (Ed.). Handbook of adolescent psychology (pp. 3-46). New York: John Wiley & Sons.

Elkind, D. (1970). Children and adolescents: Interpretive essays on Jean Piaget. New York: Oxford University Press.

Erikson, E. (1968). Identity, youth and crisis. New York: W. W. Norton.

Eveslage-Scott-T. (1997). Trash talking: Discourse and masculinity on a Boys' High School Basketball Team. American Sociological Association (Association Paper).

Falcon, Luis M. & Melendez, Edwin (1993). The Role of social networks in the labor market outcomes of Latinos, blacks and non Hispanic Whites. Study for Boston Conference on Inequality.

Farlekas, Chris. "Leander is a quiet hero." (June 18, 1994). The Times Herald Record, (p. 25).

Fine, Michelle (1977). Theorizing spaces and identities. Draft Paper.

Franklin, Anderson J. (1992). Therapy with African American men. Families in society: The Journal of Contemporary Human Services, pp. 350-55.

Franklin, Anderson J. (1993). The invisibility syndrome. The Family Therapy Networker, July/August, 33-39.

Franklin, Anderson J. and Jackson, James S. (1992). Factors contributing to positive mental health among black Americans. Handbook on Black Health & Mental Health. CT: Greenwich Press.

Fraser, George (1994). Success runs in our race: The complete guide to effective networking in the African American community. New York: William Morrow.

Frey, Darcy (1994). The Last Shot. New York: Touchstone

Furstenberg, Jr., Frank F. & Hughes, Mary Elizabeth (1995). Social capital and successful development among at-risk youth. Journal of Marriage and the Family. 57 (August 1995) 580-592.

Gans, Herbert. (1962). The urban villagers. New York: The Free Press.
Garbarino, James, Dubrow, Nancy, Kostelny, Kathleen & Pardo, Carole. (1992). Children in danger: Coping with the consequences of community violence. San Francisco: Jossey-Bass Publishers.
Garmezy, N. (1991). Resiliency and vulnerability to adverse developmental outcomes associated with poverty. American Behavioral Scientist, 34(4), 416-430.
Garmezy, Norman, Masten, Ann S. & Tellegen, Duke (1984). The study of stress and competence in children: A building block for developmental psychopathology. Child Development, 55 pp. 97-111.
Gary, Lawrence (1981). Black men. Beverly Hills, California: Sage Publications.
Gates, Louis, Jr. (1994). Colored people. New York: Knopft.
Gibbs, Nancy. (1994, June 20). The vicious cycle. Time, pp. 25-32.
Giddens, Anthony & Held, David (Eds.) (1982). Class, power and conflict: Classical and contemporary debates. Berkeley, CA: University of California Press.
Gilmore, Mikal. (1994). Shot in the heart. New York: Doubleday.
Ginott, Hasm Dr. (1969). Between parent & teenager. New York: Avon Books.
Graham, S. (1988). Can attribution theory tell us something about motivation in blacks? Educational Psychologist, 23, 3-21.
Granovetter, M. (1982). The strength of weak ties: A network theory revisited. In Marsden, P. V. & Lin, N. (eds.) Social structure and network analysis, pp. 105-130, Beverly Hills: Sage Publications.
Gunn, J.B., Duncan, Greg J. & Klebanou, Pamela Kato (1993). Do Neighborhoods Influence Child and Adolescent Development? American Journal of Sociology, 99, pp. 353-385.
Hall, G. S. (1904). Adolescence: Its psychology and its relations to physiology, anthropology, sociology, sex, crime, religion and education (2 vols.). New York: D. appleton and Company.
Hallman, Howard W. (1984). Neighborhoods: Their place in urban life. Beverly Hills, London: Sage Publications.
Hammer, Robert B. & Green, Gary P. (1994). Social Capital and Multiplexity in Relationships: Evidence from the Greater Atlanta Neighborhood Study. Study for the Russell Sage Foundation and Ford Foundation.
Hannerz, Ulf. (1969). Soulside. USA: Columbia University Press.
Hare, Bruce (1979). Black girls: A comparative analysis of self perception and achievement by race, sex and socio economic background. Baltimore: John Hopkins Univ. Center for Social Change.
Heider, F. (1958). The psychology of interpersonal relations. New York: John Wiley.
Heiss, Jerold (1994). Effects of African American family structure on school attitudes and performance. Sociological Inquiry, 67, 247-253.
Herbert, Bob (1994). "Who will help the black man in America?" The New York Times Magazine. Decembr 4, 1994.
Hill, Napoleon, (1988). Think & grow rich. New York: Ballantine Books.
Hill, Robert (1978). "The illusion of black progress." Washington, DC: National Urban League.
Hummon, David M. (1989). House, home and identity in contemporary American culture. In Setha M. Low and Erve Chambers (Eds.). Housing culture and design. PA: University of Pennsylvania Press.
Hunter, Albert. (1974). Symbolic communities: The persistence and change of Chicago's local communities. Chicago: The University of Chicago Press.
Hyram, George (1972). Challenge to society: The education of the culturally disadvantaged child. Brooklyn, NY: Pageant Poseidon.
"Inner-city kids: Outside American Dream". (June 19, 1994). The Times Herald Record, pp. 40.
Jablonsky, Thomas J. (1993). Pride in the jungle: Community and everyday life in back of the yards Chicago. Baltimore and London: The John Hopkins University Press.

Jackson, J. S. McCullough, W. R. & Gurin G. (1987). Family socialization environment and identity development in black Americans. In H. P. McAdoo (Ed.). Black families (2nd ed). Newbury Park, CA: Sage Publications.

Jacobs, Alfred & Spradlin, Wilford W. (1974). The group as agent of change. New York: Behavioral Publications.

Jencks, C., and Mayers, S.E. (1990). The social consequence of growing up in a poor neighborhood. In Lynn, L. E. McGeary, M. G. H. (eds.), Inner city poverty in the United States, pp. 111-186. Washington, D.C.: National Academy Press

Jessor, Richard, Colby, Anne and Schewder, Richard (Eds.) (1994) Neighborhood social organization: A forgotten object of ethnographic study? Essays on Ethnography and Human Development, 68 pp. 1-26.

Jones, Reginald L. (Ed.). (1980). Black psychology. New York: Harper & Row.

Kahl, Joseph. (1967). The American class structure. NY: Holt, Rinehart & Winston.

Kaplan, S. (1983). A model of person-environment compatibility. Environment and Behavior, 15, 311-332.

Kornblum, William & Williams, Terry M. (1985). Growing up poor. New York: Lexington Books.

Kotlowitz, Alex. (1991). There are no children here: The story of two boys growing up in the other America. New York: Doubleday.

Kott, J. F. (1977). Rites of passage: adolescence in America, 1790 to the present. New York: Basic Books.

Kunkel, Fritz & Dickerson, Roy E. (1947). How character develops: A psychological interpretation. New York, London: Charles Scribners.

Ladd, F. C. (1970). Black youths view their environment: Neighborhood maps. Environment and Behavior, 2, 74-99.

Ladner, J. A. (1972) Tomorrow's tomorrow. New York: Anchor Books.

Lamar, Jake. (1991). I dream a world: Portraits of black women who changed America. New York: Stewart, Tabori & Chang Inc.

Landry, Bart (1987). The new black middle class. Berkley: University of California Press.

Leadbeater, Ross, Bonnie R. and Way, Noble (Eds.) (1996). Urban girls resisting stereotypes: Creating identities. New York, London: NY University Press.

Lestor, David & Charles C. (1995). A physiological basis for personality traits: A new theory of personality. Springfield, Illinois: Thomas Publishers.

Lewin, K. (1935). A dynamic theory of personality: Selected papers. New York, London: McGraw Hill.

Lewin, K. (1943). Defining the "field at a given time." Psychological Review, 50, 292-310.

Lewin, K. (1939). Field theory and experiment in social psychology: Concepts and methods. American Journal of Sociology, 44, 868-896.

Lewin, K. (1951). Field theory in social science. New York: Harper & Row.

Lewin, K. (1936). Principles of topological psychology, (trans. F. Heider & G. M. Heider). New York: McGraw-Hill.

Lewis, Reginald F. (1995). Why should White guys have all the fun: How Reginald Lewis created a billion dollar business empire. New York: Wiley Publishers.

Liebow, Elliot. (1967). Tally's corner: A study of Negro streeetcorner men. USA: Little Brown & Company.

Lightfoot, Sara Lawrence (1983). The good high school: Portraits of character and culture. New York: Basic Books, Inc.

Lightfoot, Sara Lawrence (1994). I've known rivers: Lives of loss and liberation. New York: Addison-Wesley Publishing.

Lindsey, Gardner, Hall, Calvin S., Manosewitz, Martin, (Eds.) (1973). Theories of personality: Sources and research. New York, London, Toronto: John Wiley & Sons Inc.

Loree, Ray M. (1970). Psychology of education, (2nd ed.). New York: The Ronald Press Company.

MacLeod, Jay (1987). Ain't no making it: Aspirations & attainment in a low income neighborhood. San Francisco: Oxford Westview Press.

Madhubuti, Haki R. (1990). Black men: Obsolete, single, dangerous? The Afrikan American family in transition. Chicago: Third World Press. Brace Jovanich College Publishers.

Majors, Richard & Bilson, Janet Mancini. (1992). Cool pose: The dilemmas of black manhood in America. New York: Lexington Books.

Maurer, R. & Baxter J. C. (1972). Images of the neighborhood and city among black-Anglo and Mexican children. Environment and Behavior, 4, 351-388.

McAdoo, Harriette Pipes & John Lewis (1985). Black children: Social, educational, and parental Environments.. Newbury Park, CA: Sage Publications

McKenzie, Roderick Duncan. (1923). The neighborhood: A study of local life in the city of Columbus Ohio. Chicago: University of Chicago Press.

Melton, G. B. (1983). Toward personhood for adolescents: Autonoy and privacy as values in public policy. American Psychologist, 38, 99-103.

Miles, Michael B. & Huberman, Michael A. Qualitative data analysis.

Mincy, Ronald B. (Ed.) (1994). Nurturing young black males. Washington, DC: The Urban Institute Press.

Monroe, Sylvester (1988). Brothers: black and poor: A true story of courage and survival. New York: William Morrow and Company, Inc.

Muuss, R. E. (1982). Theories of adolescence (4 ed.). New York: Random House, [from Aristotle to the present].

Norman, Michael. (1993, December). Officer Jett's Laboratory. The New York Times Magazine, pp. 62-69.

Ogbu J. U. (1981). Origins of human competence: A cultural-ecological perspective. Child Development, 52, 413-429.

Oliver, Melvin L. & Shapiro, Thomas M. (Eds.) (1995). Black wealth/White wealth: A new perspective on racial inequality. NY & London: Routledge Press.

Powledge, Fred (1967). To change a child: A report on the Institute for Developmental Studies. Chicago: Quadrangle Books.

Pratt, Stephen R. (1989). Contrasting leadership styles and organizational effectiveness: The case of athletic teams. Social Science Quarterly, 70, 311-322.

Proctor, Samuel DeWitt (1995). The Substance of things hoped for: A memoir of African-American faith. New York: G.P. Putnam & Sons.

Proshansky, H. M. Fabian, A. K. Kaminoff, R. (1983). Place-identity: Physical world socialization of the self. Journal of Environmental Psychology, 3, 57-83.

Putnam, R. D. (1995). Bowling alone: America's declining social capital. Journal of Democracy, (1), 65-78.

Reid, Pamela Trotman & Robinson, W. La Vome. (1985). Professional black men and women: Attainment of terminal academic degrees. Psychological Reports, 56, 547-555.

Rivlin, Leanne G. (1987). Group membership and place meaning in an urban neighborhood. In Alton A. Waldersman's Neighborhood and community environments. NY: Plenum Press.

Rivlin, Leanne G. (1987). The neighborhood, personal identity and group affiliations. In Altman A. Wandersman (Ed.), Neighborhood and community environments. New York: Plenum Press.

Rodney, Walter. (1990). Walter Rodney speaks: The making of an African intellectual. Trenton, New Jersey: Africa World Press Inc.

Rutter, M. (1989). Pathways from childhood to adult life. Journal of Child Psychology and Psychiatry, 30(1), 23-51.

Ryan, Micheal. (1994, May 22). Why people fail--And why they don't. Parade Magazine, 132, pp. 4-6.

Sampson, Edward E. (1991). Social world's: Personal lives: An introduction to social psychology. Chicago, San Diego, London: Hartcourt Brace Jovanovich Publishers.

Sampson, R. J. (1991). Linking the micro and macro level dimensions of community social organization. Social Forces. 70 pp. 43-64.

Sampson, Robert J. (1993). Family and community-level influences on crime: A contextual theory and strategies for research testing. Reprint from Integrating Individual and Ecological Aspects of Crime (BRA-report).

Sandell, Jillian (1995). Out of the ghetto and into the marketplace: Hoop dreams and the commodification of marginality. Socialist Review, 25, 57-82.

Schofield, Janet W. & Anderson, Karen (1988). Chapter 13. Combining quantitative and qualitative components of research on ethnic identity and intergroup relations. The Canadian Review of Sociology and Anthropology. 25, pp. 560-76.

Shaffer, Carolyn R. and Anundsen, Kristin. (1993). Creating community anywhere: Finding support and connection in a fragmented world. New York: Putnam Publishing.

Shakur, Sanyika. (1993). The autobiography of an L.A. gang member. New York: The Atlantic Monthly Press.

Skols, D. & Shumaker, S. A. (1981). People in places: A transactional view of settings. New York: Wiley Publishers.

Spradley, James P. (1979). The ethnographic interview. Fort Worth, Philadelphia, San Diego, New York: Harcourt Brace Publishers.

Spurlock, J. (1986). Development of self concept in Afro-American children. Hospital and Community Psychology, 37, 66-70.

Staples, Robert and Johnson, Leanor Boulin. (1993). Black families at the crossroads: Challenges and prospects. San Francisco: Jossey Bass Publishers.

Stelle, Shelby. (1990). The content of our character: A new vision of race in America. USA: Harper.

Swingle, Paul G. (Ed.) (1973). Social psychology in natural settings: A reader in field experimentation. Chicago: Aldine Publishing.

Thibaut, John W. & Kelley, Harold H. (1986). The Social psychology of groups. New Brunswick: Transaction Books.

Tolman, E. C. (1932). Proposive behavior in animals and men. New York, Apleton-Century-Crafts.

Wapner, S. Kaplan, B. & Ciottone, R. (1981). Self world relationships in critical environmental transitions: Childhood and beyond. In L. S. Liben, A. H. Patterson, & N. Newcombe (Eds.). Spatial representation and behavior across the life span: Theory and application, (pp. 251-282). New York: Academic Press.

Ward, Martha Cooperfield (1982). Them children: A study in language learning. New York: Irvington Publishers.

Washington, Valora and LaPoint, Velma (1988). Black children and American institutions. New York and London: Garland Publishing, Inc.

Weiss, Robert, S. (1994). Learning from strangers: the art and method of qualitative interview studies. New York: The Free Press.

Wellman, David. (1977). Portraits of White racism. Cambridge: Cambridge University Press.

Whetstone, Muriel L. (1994, January). From the jailhouse to the statehouse. Ebony Magazine, pp. 76-78.

Whyte, William Foote (1943). Street corner society. Chicago: University of Chicago Press.

Whyte, William Foote (1955). Street corner society: The social structure of an Italian slum. Chicago: University Press.

Wigfield, Allan (1992). The development of achievement talk values: A theoretical analysis. Developmental Review, 12, 265-310.

Williams, Terry & Kornblum, W. (1986). Growing up poor. Boston: D.C. Heath.

Wilson, Julius (1978). The declining significance of race. Chicago: University of Chicago Press.

Wilson, Julius (1987). The truly disadvantaged. Chicago: University of Chicago Press.

Wolf, J. (1978). Childhood and privacy. In I. Altman & J. F. Wohlwill (Eds.), Children and the environment, (pp. 175-222). New York: Plenum Press.